THE YEAR IN TENNIS 2002

Text by Neil Harman
The International Tennis Federation
Universe

First published in the United States of America in 2003
by UNIVERSE PUBLISHING, A Division of Rizzoli International
Publications, Inc., 300 Park Avenue South, New York, NY 10010

© 2002 The International Tennis Federation, Bank Lane,
Roehampton, London, SW15 5XZ, England

2003 2004 2005 2006 / 10 9 8 7 6 5 4 3 2 1
ISBN: 0-7893-0839-8

Designed by **One** London

Printed in England

CONTENTS

The 2002 Davis Cup by BNP Paribas will be remembered as a year of firsts. In a dramatic final, Russia won its first Davis Cup title, defeating defending champion France to become only the eleventh nation to win the Cup in its 102-year history. For the first time in ninety Davis Cup Finals, a player came back from two sets to love down to win the deciding rubber. This player, twenty-year-old Mikhail Youzhny won his first live rubber to seal Russia's victory. His twenty-year-old opponent, Paul-Henri Mathieu, was making his first appearance for France.

With stories such as these, is it any wonder that the competition continues to fire the imagination of both players and fans. In fact the 2002 competition saw a record attendance of almost 600,000 spectators during the year, with over 400,000 attending the fifteen World Group ties alone. Viewers in over 170 countries watched Davis Cup on television throughout the year, and in France, a peak audience of over eight million viewed the final. The official Davis Cup website continues to grow in popularity, with the final posting a record-breaking thirty-two million page views.

However it is the performances of the players that remains the key to the success of Davis Cup. In 2002, eighteen of the world's top twenty were represented among the 541 competitors that contested the World Group and four regional Zones. From the first round through to the final, these players kept audiences on the edge of their seats, with nail-biting triumphs and losses, individual heroics and some superb tennis.

The highs and lows of this year's competition have included Sweden's fight-back in Great Britain; France's last-gasp victory over the Czech Republic; Argentina's run to the semifinals for the first time in twelve years; a record-breaking six-hour-twenty-minute doubles rubber during the Moscow semifinal; and Russia's extraordinary comeback in the final.

Sporting fans throughout the world will enjoy the special insight into the competition provided by the book. My congratulations go to our author, Neil Harman, who has completed his third edition of the Davis Cup Yearbook. He has undertaken extensive research and carried out numerous interviews to compile a comprehensive record of the Davis Cup year. His words are accompanied by some wonderful photographs that we have received from the best tennis photographers in the world.

My congratulations go to Russia for their first title after two previous final defeats. I must also recognize the tremendous achievement of France in reaching a third final in four years and maintaining their position atop the ITF Davis Cup Nations Ranking. I would like to recognize all 142 nations who entered this year and wish each nation well in their campaign for the 2003 Davis Cup.

Francesco Ricci Bitti
President
International Tennis Federation

PRESIDENT'S MESSAGE

FOREWORD

Dear Friends,

I am very pleased to write this welcome message. As you know Russia won its first-ever Davis Cup title. I want to congratulate all my team, all the players – we deserve it. It is a weekend that will stay in many people's memories for a very long time.

The Davis Cup is a very special competition in tennis as well as in the whole of international sport, as it is a team competition. I think there is no greater honor for an athlete than to represent his country. Everybody is watching you. They want you to win. It is really difficult, you know, to fight against the player, against the crowd. But I did everything in the best interests of the team and I am proud of what I did. When I was listening to our national anthem and all players were on the court facing the flag, I felt my heart beating. And I like this feeling. The Davis Cup trophy is ours.

If somebody asks me to list the best and worst moments in my life, I guess the Davis Cup will play its part. There are some specific moments in playing tennis when you understand how much your life depends on this yellow ball. Some players can reconcile the pressure, some players cannot, but everybody leaves the court more experienced and full of unforgettable memories. Playing Davis Cup can help an athlete discover so many unexpected qualities. Also, the support, it means a lot. It is the first time we had so many fans, Russian fans, while playing abroad.

I feel a part of the Davis Cup as I represent Russia on court. Now the Russian team is part of Davis Cup history and I hope it is able to keep this famous silver trophy.

Yours sincerely

Yevgeny Kafelnikov

INTRODUCTION

Every year, someone somewhere gets the Davis Cup kick for the first time. Even those who have been around the block once or twice—or whose career in the competition never extended beyond their induction—remember "the first time." It's that sudden inability to sleep, an odd tightening of the stomach muscles, a severe outbreak of sweaty palms, or the nauseous feeling when your head and your legs don't seem to be yours.

It is a reminder of just what makes the competition so special and why, after ninety finals across 102 years, it still holds us in a thrall that Dwight Davis would surely have found appreciably unnerving. What started as a philanthropic bash between a couple of friendly foes, the United States and Great Britain, has spread its wings with a boundless energy so that it now encompasses 142 nations.

Those of us watching these brave men, with only a racket or six with which to defend their cause, marvel that they have do not faint on court when the umpire flicks the coin into the air. This year we saw one of those rarities of the Cup, a singles debut in the final. Paul-Henri Mathieu of France strode out to take his place in the annals of the Davis Cup's abundant history. The fifth such player since the Challenge Round was abolished in 1971, he stood his corner without once suggesting he was troubled by the prospect. Only with the final result—one of glorious unpredictability for which the event is famed—did he give in to the emotions coursing through his veins. He will come back a stronger, better man.

Three other players made their World Group singles debuts in the 2002 competition, now sponsored with the proper mixture of innovation and care by BNP Paribas. Scott Draper of Australia played his first match in the opening round of the World Group in Argentina, Spain's Tommy Robredo played on grass in Houston against the United States, which was a novelty in itself; and two months after he had played in his first Wimbledon final, Argentina's David Nalbandian was granted his first Cup experience in the semifinals against Russia. None of the three managed a singles win, emphasizing the monstrous burden of "the first time."

Fabrice Santoro has completed a dozen years playing for France, and yet he can recall the first occasion with absolute clarity. He suffered a straight-sets defeat to Australia's Richard Fromberg in the second rubber of a World Group Quarterfinal in Nimes in 1991, followed by victory over Wally Masur in the fifth that clinched the tie for his country. He was borne around the stadium that Sunday afternoon on the shoulders of the captain Yannick Noah. How could a sporting life improve after that?

"The hardest thing is to play a Davis Cup match when you're not ready, because then you start to ask yourself questions and you can completely miss your match," he said. "What happened to me in Nimes was something so special, so magical. You do not know how you are going to perform and then you are transported to a level beyond your imagination."

OPPOSITE: Mikhail Youzhny (RUS)
ABOVE: Paul-Henri Mathieu (FRA)

This could become the motif of the Davis Cup. It is an event that transports us all to levels beyond our imagination. Can it get better than Paris 2002? Let us wait for 2003 before making a judgment. As such, cries for change in the competition's format have all but ceased. Only in America—an irony given the nationality of the man who inspired the event—is the call for "modernization" a touch too strident. But the current captain of the U.S. team, Patrick McEnroe, is not one of the change-for-the-sake-of-change brigade.

"You come here," said McEnroe, after the 3–2 defeat in the semifinals to France at Roland Garros, "and see what the Cup is all about and you wonder 'if it's a problem for America, so what?' It is almost like—is it worth it to change? Could the event be any better from a fan's perspective? If the U.S. public can't catch on to that, well, too bad." Whether such words would be the mantra of the United States Tennis Association is a matter of conjecture but in terms of how the Davis Cup is viewed outside the fifty states, McEnroe spoke a telling truth.

Of course, there are not only players and journalists who have a Davis Cup story to tell about "the first time." Let us not overlook the officials. Bruno Rebeuh of France made his debut as a chair umpire at the Monaco versus Zimbabwe Euro/African Zone Group I tie in the Principality in 1982. His abiding memory of it is that the Monaco authorities could not lay their hands on a tape of the Zimbabwean national anthem so the team captain said he would teach his players the words within a couple of days. They sang it, unaccompanied, at the opening ceremony.

Rebeuh went on to umpire ten finals. The one that springs most vividly to his mind is the 1992 affair between the United States and Switzerland in Forth Worth, Texas. "The Americans had Agassi, Courier, Sampras, and McEnroe, and everyone thought it was going to be a one-sided affair. Then (Marc) Rosset defeated Courier in the second singles, so it was 1–1 and the Swiss led the doubles against McEnroe and Sampras by two sets to love. You can imagine how difficult it became to umpire.

"And people should not forget how much pressure is on the umpire and linespeople at every tie. At a Grand Slam, you have the qualifying matches, the early rounds, and if you are lucky, and you are allowed to take charge of the final, you have had ten matches to get used to everything. A neutral umpire sits in the chair on the Friday and has to be ready straight away. The grand slams are a piece of cake compared to Davis Cup."

Watching Britain's Mike Morrissey repeatedly, pleadingly calling to order the supporters of France and Russia in the final, one was reminded of the integrity of the neutral in these momentous ties. When everyone around him is in danger of losing their faculties, the umpire has to be firm, fair, and, occasionally, forgiving. Morrissey was excellent.

In terms of spectator interest, there is no doubt that the Davis Cup fires everyone's imagination. From 1998, the attendance figures were as follows: 415,336 in 1998; 443,698 in 1999; 529,589 in 2000; 507,414 in 2001; and 593,704 in 2002. Could Dwight Davis really have believed such huge numbers?

As the number of hours of terrestrial television coverage grows at a healthy rate, so does the size of the cumulative audience. The 2000 television audience figure of 612 million viewers had grown to 619 million in 2001 and exceeded 640 million in 2002. The event has traditionally been strong with television audiences in Europe, but the emergence of players such as Gustavo Kuerten of Brazil (and watch for Argentina and Chile further emerging next year) has resulted in the Americas now accounting for 27% of the total television audience. The regional split was: Europe at 41%, Asia/Oceania at 27%, the Americas at 27%, and Africa at 5%.

The first Davis Cup tie I attended was the 1986 tie at Telford, England, between Great Britain and Spain, and to say that I was hooked is an understatement. The magic that first touched Davis all those years ago, the image he saw in his mind's eye and how it had grown into an event of such beauty, came together in rural Shropshire, hardly a seething hotbed of the tennis world. But Telford came alive as it has rarely done since.

Sixteen years later, as I write this book for the third year, it becomes all the more astonishing to witness the growth and development of the championship across its many boundaries. In 2002 the only member of the top twenty who did not make himself available was Andre Agassi. Lleyton Hewitt, the number one in the world, has a passion for the event that borders on the fanatical. He went on the record to say that he would be tailoring his schedule for 2003 around the four slams and the Davis Cup. It was music to the ears.

The Davis Cup has never been more popular, never been more relevant, and never looked more beautiful. As the name plates were being polished in the grand Hotel De Ville in preparation for the 2002 final draw ceremony, I was reminded of the words of I. Michael Heyman, once the secretary of the Smithsonian Institution in the United States. He said about objects that "there is a power of them, of real things, to move us in ways we can barely articulate, stimulating memory, evoking emotions."

That is the Davis Cup. Here forever to move us in all those wonderful ways.

OPPOSITE: David Nalbandian (ARG)
ABOVE: Scott Draper (AUS)

FRANCE d. NETHERLANDS 3–2 | Metz, France · indoor clay
CZECH REPUBLIC d. BRAZIL 4–1 | Ostrava, Czech Republic · indoor carpet
SPAIN d. MOROCCO 3–2 | Zaragoza, Spain · indoor clay
USA d. SLOVAK REPUBLIC 5–0 | Oklahoma City, USA · indoor hard
RUSSIA d. SWITZERLAND 3–2 | Moscow, Russia · indoor clay
SWEDEN d. GREAT BRITAIN 3–2 | Birmingham, Great Britain · indoor carpet
CROATIA d. GERMANY 4–1 | Zagreb, Croatia · indoor carpet
ARGENTINA d. AUSTRALIA 5–0 | Buenos Aires, Argentina · outdoor clay

SWEDEN CELEBRATES
AS JOHANSSON COMPLETES
DRAMATIC COMEBACK

GREAT BRITAIN V SWEDEN

The British and the Swedes had been inextricably linked from the very first in 2002. In the second round of the Australian Open, Jonas Bjorkman defeated his countryman Thomas Enqvist and then went on to snuff out British No. 1 Tim Henman, who had previously survived his own test of nerve against fellow Brit Greg Rusedski. Bjorkman subsequently lost to another Swede Thomas Johansson, who was about to stun everyone by winning the first Slam of his career.

It was around this time that a few experts in the media realized that the World Group First Round tie in the Davis Cup by BNP Paribas might not be the straightforward stroll they had hoped for. A glance at Sweden's record in the competition worsened the rumblings already felt in British stomachs.

Still out in Melbourne, Henman became saddled with the weight of home expectation once it emerged he was the highest seed left in the tournament with an excited population preparing itself to welcome him home a champion. And so, when he froze against Bjorkman—losing his first three service games and unable to choose what sort of game he should play—the angry brigade in England had a field day. The back pages of the newspapers were covered in wrath. Henman spent the week before the Davis Cup tie refusing to speak to the media, who were informed that the British side had adopted a siege mentality that would not be easily negotiated away.

Swedish Captain Carl-Axel Hageskog's side had arrived in Birmingham with the endorsement of former superstars ringing in their ears. Bjorn Borg, who normally treats newspapers as one would a scorpion with its stinger rattling, called Stockholm's evening paper, *Expressen,* to offer his congratulations to Johansson on his triumph. Stefan Edberg, another player who prefers the shy, conciliatory life, said that Johansson had done himself an enormous favor by concentrating on playing and not whining as much as he used to.

There had not been a single Swedish sports writer in Melbourne to record the twenty-six-year-old Johansson's memorable victory but the media scrum at his homecoming more than made up for their perceived lack of interest in what Swedish players were trying to achieve—and clearly succeeding. "Unusually for Sweden there has been a very good reaction and very positive feedback," said Bjorkman. "What Thomas and I achieved in Australia is a huge step and it's a lot of fun to be given the credit. The best part has been seeing names like Borg and Edberg in the papers wanting to speak about us."

"The form-guide for us is good going into the tie against Britain but both Tim (Henman) and Greg (Rusedski) have won titles also this year and if they came up a little short at the Australian Open, I still think they are both very good players."

As standard bearers of a famous legacy in Davis Cup and beyond, Hageskog had chosen Bjorkman, Johansson, Thomas Enqvist, and Magnus Larsson as his side. There was, however, an anxious moment when Johansson flew home only a day after arriving in Birmingham for a specialist's treatment for a groin problem. The draw would be fascinating.

OPPOSITE: Thomas Johansson **(TOP LEFT)** is congratulated by his Swedish teammates after defeating Britain's Greg Rusedski **(BOTTOM LEFT)** in the deciding fifth rubber. Thomas Enqvist **(RIGHT)** had earlier weighed in with two singles victories.

Johansson was back in town for the ceremony, which—at the hands of the ITF President, Francesco Ricci Bitti—pitted Henman against Bjorkman in the opener. This immediate rematch, after all that had gone on some twenty days earlier half the world away, became the focus of the tie.

Hageskog surprised everyone by naming Enqvist over Johansson as the first singles player playing Rusedski on the opening day, with the prospect of facing Henman in a potentially critical reverse singles match on Sunday. All the while Johansson sat beaming throughout the press conference—noone knew how serious his injury was.

A full house of 10,950 greeted Bjorkman to the strains of Abba's "The Winner Takes It All," whereas the British preferred Robbie Williams's "Let Me Entertain You." There was a fevered anticipation around the National Indoor Arena, which had become the spiritual home to Britain's Davis Cup hopes. Henman rose to the occasion.

The match was as intense as expected. Henman won the first two sets, but then, in an exchange of five breaks of serve in eight games, lost the third and found himself down 3-1 in the fourth when he double-faulted on a fourth break point.

Serving at 4–2, Bjorkman trailed 0–30 and the crowd was drawn from its state of nervous agitation to one of profound voice. And, unlike Melbourne, where a Swedish flag was attached to every person in five, the Swede had no one to help but his teammates on the bench. Bjorkman lost his serve to love, Henman re-focused and drove through a superb backhand winner to break for a 6-5 lead.

When Bjorkman netted a final forehand service return, Henman bent his knees in mid-court, stooped low, and drew his right hand up to his face in mimicry of the Swedish victory salute, the "Vycht." Bjorkman was not amused. "He should not have done it, that's a Swedish sign," he said. "I suppose he did it more in relief than anything."

Henman was soon on his chair courtside but could do nothing to rouse Rusedski to what would have been his most important win for Britain. Even in two tiebreaks, when the man with the fastest serve in the world might have been expected to prevail, Rusedski was found wanting against Enqvist, who gave a rock-solid performance of redoubtable defense and ferocious attack. His 7–6, 7–6, 6–2 victory brought a sense of realism to a rousing afternoon.

Sweden surprised no one when they announced that Johansson would be replacing Larsson in the doubles with Bjorkman. As always, Henman and Rusedski were paired together, defending a record of five wins out of five in the event. What followed was an uplifting experience for all but Bjorkman and Johansson. The British duo may indeed—as Bjorkman intimated—be angry rivals, but put them together in Davis Cup and someone up there sprinkles Henman and Rusedski with fistfuls of magic dust.

Henman and Rusedski may well have been inspired by Bjorkman's column in a Swedish paper on the eve of this tie. He said that Sweden is a team while Britain is not. Ironically it was Bjorkman—left desperately flailing at a backhand service return on match point—who then had to witness the bear hug between Henman and Rusedski as they celebrated a 7–6, 2–6, 6–7, 6–3, 6–3 victory.

Henman was the outstanding performer throughout. It was not until the final set that he sacrificed his serve, perhaps courtesy of two dismal backhand volleys from Rusedski littering his contribution. It would have been easy for the British pair to be unhinged by that setback, but they steadied themselves and hammered away at the Bjorkman serve that was unraveling like a cardigan snagged on a protruding nail.

The Swedes may have been worn down on this occasion, but they did not resemble a beaten team. They had been in this position before and triumphed. There was a fire in the eye of Enqvist when he stepped out to face Henman in Sunday's opening singles. In a trial of strength, the Swede would not give way, crushing the British No. 1 in straight sets, 6–4, 6–2, 6–4 in a match that took him to deuce only once on his serve. How would Rusedski now cope against the new Australian Open champion, who, as expected, was brought in for the deciding rubber?

Rusedski walked out with one arm raised, like a prizefighter, but Johansson had all the smart moves. He ducked and dived, bobbed and weaved, and even when Rusedski won the first set to an absolute din, it seemed only a matter of time before the Swede found his Melbourne groove.

When he broke the Rusedski serve with three plum returns in the eighth game of the second set, there was a cumulative sharp intake of Birmingham breath. Rusedski responded by breaking twice to lead in the third, but the little Swede responded by taking the British player's next two service games for the loss of a single point. That stretch of five games in a row was to prove decisive.

Tim Henman and Greg Rusedski **(SECOND RIGHT)** roused the home crowd **(SECOND LEFT)** with a battling five-set doubles victory, but final day wins for Thomas Enqvist **(RIGHT)** and Thomas Johansson **(LEFT)** saw Sweden home in Birmingham.

Tim Henman **(LEFT)** won two of his three rubbers for Great Britain, but it was Thomas Johansson who went on to celebrate with Swedish captain Carl-Axel Hageskog **(SECOND LEFT)**. A packed Pabellon Principe Felipe **(SECOND RIGHT)** witnessed heartbreak for Morocco's Karim Alami **(RIGHT)**, who was forced to retire in the deciding fifth rubber against Alex Corretja.

For all of Rusedski's worthy willingness, he could not hold Johansson off and Sweden registered one of the finest victories in their exceptional history in the event.

"When I saw Rusedski sprinting all over the place in the final match, I was happy because I knew Thomas was waiting and would exhaust him in the end," said Hageskog. "The British team did well but they simply ran out of steam."

The Swedish captain said that he could have picked any four from the ten players on his team and would have been perfectly satisfied. British Captain Roger Taylor knew that, come September, it was still likely he would only have the usual two to choose from.

SPAIN V MOROCCO

It had been fourteen months since Spain could actually show their fans what it was like to be a part of the World Group of Davis Cup.

As winners of the trophy—for the first time in their history—in December 2000, the team had enjoyed a level of notoriety and self-satisfaction that comes to only a few tennis players in their careers. Within two months of that momentous success in Barcelona, however, Spain had lost to Holland in the 2001 first round, without ever having enough time to enjoy the splendor of their unique triumph.

As such, returning to the elite sixteen was one thing—the next nugget was a home tie. The draw against Morocco gave the Spaniards that enticing prospect and they chose the Pabellon Principe Felipe in Zaragoza as its regal setting. Of the two teams, the Moroccans boasted the man in form while Spain was somewhat suspect. Younes El Aynaoui had won the ATP title in Doha. Spain's Juan Carlos Ferrero had been forced out of the Australian Open with a knee injury and Alex Corretja had lost in the first round to American James Blake.

The opening day would tell the tale. Ferrero certainly seemed to be in no way inhibited by his injury, swatting away the challenge of Hicham Arazi in three distinct sets in a manner richly endorsing his reputation as the prince of clay. Arazi simply could not cope with the Spaniard's infinite superiority off the ground, especially on his whipping forehand.

"There is always a little extra pressure in Davis Cup, whether you are at home or not," said Ferrero, "but today, I played an unbelievable match. I felt when I won the first two sets that he would not be able to come back. I forgot all about the problems with my knee."

If the home fans felt this was the perfect opportunity for a siesta, they had precious little time to relax. The scintillating form of El Aynaoui had been well documented. He was in great shape, whereas no one could be sure how Corretja would perform. As creditably as the Spanish talisman played, it wasn't quite good enough, as the reed-slim Moroccan was totally undaunted by whatever the crowd threw at him.

IT'S HUGE. KARIM ALAMI (MAR)

"When you play Davis Cup it's a special feeling coming from your heart. You play for your country and that's what counts.

El Aynaoui was in touch with his game from the outset, probing for signs of weakness or lack of confidence in Corretja, and taking the initiative with an aggression that his opponent found unanswerable. "He always had control of the match," Corretja was forced to confess. "I had my chances at the start of the second set, but once they weren't taken, it made a big difference. Every time he was in trouble, he came up with a nice serve or a powerful response off the ground. I just felt for me there was something missing."

El Aynaoui's 6–3, 7–5, 6–4 success brought the teams level on Friday evening and presented him with one of the most satisfying day's work of his career. For this, he felt, was not one man against one man, but one man against an entire country. Not for the first time, a Spanish sporting crowd let its enthusiasm get the better of it.

The Moroccan is such a nice guy that he didn't want to make too much of the crowd's lack of objectivity. But he could not entirely avoid commenting on it. "I never had to face anything like that before," said El Aynaoui. "It's really tough to deal with when you are missing your first serve and everyone is standing and clapping. But this is the charm of the Davis Cup. In Morocco, I suppose, it would have been the same."

The charm? Did he say "charm"? What a wonderful understatement! One that only emphasizes how difficult it is for the home fans—most of whom have been brought up on a diet of soccer—to control themselves when a national team is competing. El Aynaoui said the crowd's reactions motivated him. "I wanted to show them so much how I was the better player and I did."

"Really the World Group is something fantastic for Morocco," he said. "The match was live on television at home—we are getting great support from everybody. There are two Moroccan TV stations here and being able to be seen at home means I have this wonderful feeling I'm giving something back to the people of my country. It is always easier to identify yourself with a country than an individual."

The Spaniards would agree with that. In his 2000 foreword to this book, Alex Corretja wrote that nothing for him could match the magic of lifting the Davis Cup for the first time in the country's history. For him to lose such a match was a heavy blow, but he knew that he had less than a day to rid his system of it.

Doubles with Juan Balcells against Arazi and Karim Alami would clearly be pivotal and the Moroccans started the stronger, taking the first set 6–2 to conjure unthinkable images in the Spanish team. But the more experienced team—bulwarks of the 2000 final—kept their nerve and secured a victory that pushed Spain's noses back in front.

This was to be a tie that spread-eagled the emotions. Under the circumstances, El Aynaoui had probably never played better in his life than he did in the first reverse singles, surviving a Ferrero fightback that brought the match level at two sets all, to win 7–6, 6–0, 3–6, 0–6, 6–3. The pride of the Moroccan was evident as he leapt around the stadium with his son, Ewen, in his arms.

So what of the fifth rubber? The Moroccan captain, Amine Ghissasse, had a huge decision to make. Alami had played superbly in the doubles and had beaten Corretja twice in their seven matches, whereas Arazi had lost to him three times.

Ghissasse went with Alami but, after a tight first set went Spain's way, it was clear as the second started that the big muscular Moroccan was struggling. Having requested a medical time-out at 0-3, he tried to play on after treatment, but he was hurting. As soon as the second set was over, Alami sank to the chair, covered his head in a towel, and cried his eyes out.

"When you play Davis Cup it is a special feeling coming from your heart," he said. "You play for your country, you play for your flag, you play for your team—and that's what counts. It is huge and I am so sad today." An entire nation wept with him.

ABOVE: Younes El Aynaoui kept Morocco in the hunt against Spain with two singles victories.

OPPOSITE: Wins for Juan Carlos Ferrero (**BOTTOM LEFT**) and Juan Balcells and Alex Corretja (**RIGHT**) helped silence the Moroccan fans (**TOP LEFT**), before the tie ended in dramatic circumstances.

HEARTBREAK FOR MOROCCANS
AS SPAIN ADVANCES
TO QUARTERFINALS

DEFENDING CHAMPIONS FRANCE
SAFELY ADVANCE
TO QUARTERFINALS

FRANCE V NETHERLANDS

It had only been two months since the French were cavorting across a battered and bruised grass court at Melbourne Park, holding Nicolas Escude up to the stars, and exalting in a wonderful Davis Cup success.

Escude himself would never forget the moment. The French resources, however, were so strong that he was not even chosen by captain Guy Forget for its opening defense of the title against the Netherlands in the Northern French city of Metz.

This was a repeat of the 2001 semifinal with Escude winning a five-set marathon against Sjeng Schalken to help his country earn a place in the final. However, this year, on a slower clay court, Forget preferred to engage Arnaud Clement and Sebastien Grosjean in the singles.

There was a change in the Dutch side too. Raemon Sluiter, who limped out of the 2001 semifinal when he turned his ankle so distressingly against Clement, had not recovered sufficiently to try to sustain his otherwise charmed life in his country's colors.

The loss of Sluiter provided captain Tjerk Bogtstra with the opportunity to give Edwin Kempes his debut in the singles. But it was a tall order for the young Dutchman against the player who had ended the regular tour year in 2001 as a worthy runner-up in the Tennis Masters Cup to Lleyton Hewitt.

What did Grosjean know of his opponent? It amounted to very little, truth be told. Kempes had hardly uprooted many trees in his ATP career, but take most men out of the weekly drudge of competition and paint their face in their country's colors, and they become inspired to soaring heights.

Grosjean took the opening set, but the Dutchman led 5–3 in the second and was only two points from tying the match up. It was here that Grosjean was able to raise his game to heights his opponent had not touched in his career. Just when the French team needed him, Grosjean came hurtling through, winning the second set in a tiebreak and racing through the third in thirty-four minutes for a 7–5, 7–6, 6–2 victory.

To be fair to Kempes, he gave his best—but it just wasn't good enough against the more experienced Grosjean. "I was a little bit nervous because I can't say I had seen too much of him," said Grosjean. "I had to play well because he played well. When he was winning, it inspired me to play that little bit better. I think the experience of playing a singles first in the Davis Cup was also an important thing for me to have."

Arnaud Clement had been a spectator in the 2001 final in Melbourne, a situation that must have been hard to swallow for the little guy who had reached the final of the Australian Open in the same stadium ten months earlier. Clement rightly shared in the glory but there must have been a slightly hollow ring to his personal celebration.

OPPOSITE: Sebastien Grosjean **(LEFT)** and Arnaud Clement **(TOP RIGHT)** helped France make a winning start to its title defense under the watchful eye of captain Guy Forget **(BOTTOM RIGHT)**.

ABOVE: Dutchman Sjeng Schalken (LEFT) partnered Paul Haarhuis (CENTER) to a doubles victory against France, but suffered five-set singles defeats against both Arnaud Clement (RIGHT) and Sebastien Grosjean.

OPPOSITE: Guillermo Canas came from behind against Scott Draper to give Argentina a 1–0 lead in Buenos Aires.

So when Forget called him in as second singles in Metz, there was more on the line than just a simple tennis match. Clement wanted to prove he was worthy of selection. He had been instrumental in their semifinal victory over the Dutch the previous year and believed he had the number of anyone in the side.

This tie pitted him against Sjeng Schalken, a player for whom this competition does something very special. There is something of the soldier about him in Davis Cup, a courageous guardsman who will not give in until he reaches his final round of ammunition. His match with Clement was to be a minor classic.

From a set up, Clement was taken aback by Schalken's riposte, a characteristically sweet spell of hitting that took him into the lead by two sets to one. The momentum was in a constant state of flux for four hours until finally Clement prevailed in the fifth set.

"It was very tough today," he said afterward. "I had a good chance in the third set but then got nervous and didn't finish it off as I should. But I have a lot of confidence in my physical ability in the final set of matches. It is important to know you have a good chance of winning the match. That is what makes me tough."

The Dutch, therefore, had to win the doubles to keep themselves afloat and it was no surprise that Bogtstra should turn to the perennial Paul Haarhuis to partner Schalken. They did not let him down. The Cedric Pioline–Fabrice Santoro pairing that had twisted the knife against Australia in the 2001 final after they had defeated Haarhuis and Schalken in the semis, could not rediscover that edge this year. The veteran Haarhuis, who had held off retirement to chase Davis Cup glory, became the key figure, especially as the fourth set came down to the wire. The Dutch pair saved three set points at 3-5 down and set off on a roll of four successive games to take the match.

This left Grosjean with the responsibility of seeing his nation through—a responsibility he did not shirk. Indeed, he performed heroics against Schalken, who led 2–0 in the fifth set but could not raise himself to triumph in what was his second five-setter in a row and third match in successive days. "I feel so wonderful, I can hardly explain it," said Grosjean. "The joy I am feeling is both personal and for the whole team. I was being dominated and the crowd woke me up and pushed me all the way. This is a great satisfaction for this tie and for my whole career."

ARGENTINA V AUSTRALIA

When the draw for the 2002 World Group was announced, John Fitzgerald could have been forgiven for believing the fates had not dealt him the kind of hand a man of his character deserved.

Still reeling from the levels of vitriol against his selections in the 2001 final, he now had to pick his way through a tie in Buenos Aires that was bound to be fraught with difficulties.

Patrick Rafter had "retired," or so he insisted. Mark Philippoussis was nowhere near fit or confident enough to be plunged back into Davis Cup. And just for desperately bad measure, Lleyton Hewitt had suddenly come out in a nasty rash.

During the Hopman Cup in Perth (the first week of the year), the newly crowned world No. 1 was discovered to have contracted chicken pox. Right away, he had to be quarantined. Unless this remarkable young man could shake off the effects quickly, Fitzgerald knew he might well have to go to Argentina with a diminished squad.

Neither Hewitt's condition nor his equability had eased by the time of the Australian Open, where he lost at Rod Laver Arena in the first round to Alberto Martin of Spain. For the first time in his career, people truly felt for him. He sat through the rest of the tournament supporting his girlfriend Kim Clijsters, wrapped in his sweatshirt like a refugee from a hospital ward. It was not a good omen for Argentina.

Fitzgerald kept a straight face, exuding optimism as only he can, but he was fast becoming reduced to the most meager of resources. Eventually, he chose Scott Draper, who had never played a Davis Cup singles in his life, and the combustible Romanian-born Andrew Ilie, also a first-timer. After having the Cup ripped from his grasp in December, Fitzgerald now had to field a completely novice team six weeks later. Did tennis get more unyielding than this?

Having played twenty-three ties in ten years, Todd Woodbridge was the elder statesman of the side and knew that his influence on the squad was going to be vital. "Australia has had three excellent years in the event, winning it in 1999, losing the final in 2000 and again last year," he said. "Now we are coming into a tie in which we're clearly the underdogs. They have a full strength side and we have a few of our stars missing. For the first time in my career, I'm the leader of the team so I have to draw on that and share it with my teammates."

The Argentines, by comparison, were celebrating their return to the World Group for the first time in a decade. And what better place to relish such a renaissance than at home, on clay (their favored surface), against a nation shorn of its finest by injury, illness, and retirement? If they lost this tie, there would surely be hell to pay.

When they entered the court at the quaintly named Buenos Aires Lawn Tennis Club, the team was dressed in the famed blue-and-white standard of the Argentine soccer team. Nothing could have done more to rouse the near full house drawn to the arena to witness what was expected to be a fairly one-sided affair.

Draper, who had recovered from the sad death of his wife with a wonderful attitude about life, was first up against the world No. 15, Guillermo Canas. There was no way Draper would allow himself to be swallowed up: when he came back from losing the first set to lead by two sets to one and 2-1 in the fourth, the green and gold supporters were suddenly contemplating something they had dared not believe.

Canas needed all of his daring and confidence to hang onto the match. At the moment of direst need, however, he came up with the attacking shots, moving forward into the position you might have expected Draper to occupy. Gradually, as the crowd's influence grew, so did the confidence of Canas—

"You feel like you are in paradise. After you finish the third point, and the people that support you come in to celebrate, **IT IS A SENSATION** that you only have in the Davis Cup"

GUILLERMO CANAS (ARG)

he managed to eke out the last two sets, securing the victory that was to have enormous meaning to his country.

Ilie had talked often about his desire to play Davis Cup. The shirt-ripping, histrionic Ilie had won an enormous fan club both inside and outside Australia, but it remained to be seen if his expansive character was the right fit for the competition. Gaston Gaudio simply didn't give him a chance.

Ilie had not even gotten started before Gaudio was well on his way to the 6–1, 6–1, 6–2 victory that aptly summed up Fitzgerald's worst fears about the tie. "Gaston was so consistent," said Fitzgerald's opposite number, Alejandro Gattiker. "Everything went right for him, he was moving well, striking the ball brilliantly, short angles, heavy shots, drop shots. It was a great match from him."

With one win from three matches needed to secure Argentina's victory, the atmosphere grew to a fevered pitch—not unlike an Argentine soccer match. Not even a two-hour rain delay could dampen the crowd's enthusiasm. The doubles would conspire to be one of the all-time classic Davis Cup matches.

Todd Woodbridge had played in the competition for a decade but the hurt of being left out of the doubles in the previous year's final against France still ran deep. He felt he could have done better with either of the chosen pairing of Hewitt or Rafter but had to accept the captain's decision with as much grace as he could muster. The travails of Wayne Arthurs, chosen to be his partner in Buenos Aires, had been well documented. Who could possibly forget the picture of him in tears after the fifth and deciding match in Melbourne?

Together, they had awful memories to erase, whereas Argentina's team of Canas and Lucas Arnold had no such baggage to carry. They just wanted to go out there and win the tie. Emotions went through the wringer during three-and-a-half hours of tennis of epic proportions. Argentina came from behind to lead by two sets to one, only for Arthurs and Woodbridge to power back and take the fourth 6–1.

The fifth set was often too tense to watch, let alone to participate in, but there was always a sense that Argentina had the edge. Arnold was the rock, Canas more full of flair, and the crowd could not contain its allegiance. In the end, the home side prevailed 10–8. The tie was over and Arthurs was in despair again.

As the champagne sprayed over him, it was left to Canas to explain exactly what this victory meant. "After we finished the third point and the people came out to celebrate it was a wonderful feeling. This is a sensation you can only have in the Davis Cup. You feel as if you are in paradise."

ABOVE: Scott Draper battled hard on his debut but went down in five sets to Guillermo Canas.

OPPOSITE: After Gaston Gaudio **(TOP RIGHT)** overwhelmed Andrew Ilie, Canas **(LEFT)** went on to celebrate a five-set doubles victory with Lucas Arnold **(BOTTOM RIGHT)**.

ARGENTINA ADVANCES WITH CLEAN SWEEP OVER AUSTRALIA

USA V SLOVAK REPUBLIC

When Pete Sampras decided at the start of 2002 that the Davis Cup really meant something to him again, the American captain Patrick McEnroe was understandably torn.

Having come clear-eyed into the job, nailing his colors so understandably to the promise of Andy Roddick and James Blake, what was McEnroe to do? Should he simply bow to Sampras's greater wealth of experience? Or stand true to the teenagers who had driven America back to the World Group in what had been a tumultuous year for the nation?

The fact that America had drawn the Slovak Republic at home in the opening round could have helped convince McEnroe. After all, it was not expected to be a difficult tie, whichever players he selected. And he had better not antagonize Sampras, who had more than once held his nation's Davis Cup's dream together.

"Patrick (McEnroe) brings a lot of good energy," Sampras said. "He has a personality that can mold lots of types of players. He knows my game well, he has a nice easy-going personality, and he knows each player in his different way and that's my definition of a good captain, someone who is able to see the situation and be able to adjust to it."

We've played quite a bit of Davis Cup over the years and I think it's something I could really use to my advantage. It does mean something when you're playing for your country and your teammates. You go out there, you dig a little deeper and you push a little harder. There's a renewed sense of urgency when you play Davis Cup."

As he looked around at the Slovak team assembled on the other side of the draw table, Sampras must have wondered just what had happened to the competition in the time he'd been away. Who were these guys? Karol Kucera and Dominik Hrbaty had been the mainstays of Slovak tennis since Czechoslovakia had split into two. But both were suffering: Kucera's spine was causing him difficulties and Hrbaty had a strained Achilles tendon. And so Miloslav Mecir, the captain, was forced to field a novice combination in Jan Kroslak and nineteen-year-old Karol Beck, ranked a place apart at No. 269 and 268 respectively.

Mecir said: "For many years, we played with those guys. I think it was almost a miracle that no one was injured during the Davis Cup. It's a pity for the both of them that at the same time now they got injured. Dominik has been injured for a long time. He had problems at the Australian Open and when he came back he still had inflammation and he didn't want to take the risk to make it even worse. Karol was practicing the Thursday before we left and then decided it was hurting him more and he was not well enough to continue. We will do the best we can."

The choice of venue was a sensitive one. Oklahoma City had been through tough times of its own, what with the bombing of the Alfred P. Murrah Federal Building in April of 1995 that had caused 168 deaths and so much pain and heartache. America was hurting again after the terrorist attacks of the

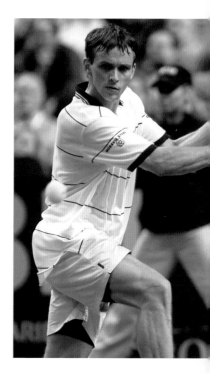

OPPOSITE: Andy Roddick (TOP LEFT) and James Blake (RIGHT) helped the United States to victory over the Slovak Republic to the delight of the home fans (BOTTOM LEFT).

ABOVE: Jan Kroslak put up a battling performance in his four-set defeat by Roddick.

11th of September and so sport and spirit were joined together in powerful unity. It would prove an unstoppable combination.

Sampras was the elder statesman of the U.S.A. side, McEnroe having brought in another of the promising teenagers, Mardy Fish, in preference to Todd Martin in the doubles. A crowd of 6,500 in the Myriad Convention Center was the highest ever for a first round tie in the United States. Sampras played Beck, which, anywhere else, would have seemed little short of a mismatch. Not in Davis Cup—an event to which the United States was to be given a rude reawakening.

The first set was routine enough, but Beck, who had never played above challenger status on the ATP Tour, was not to be intimidated, striking back to take the second on a tiebreak. The Oklahoma crowd had not been ready to see their hero so flustered. Beck let the moment go to his head temporarily—and it may well have cost him the match.

Sampras came bouncing back to take the third 6–1 but even then Beck was a break up in the fourth before the older man prevailed. "He came out swinging away and played a great match, so you have to give him credit," said Sampras. "He's one to watch. There were one or two anxious moments and I definitely had to work hard to come through. It was one of those days where I just didn't quite have my rhythm, like a baseball pitcher not having his fastball."

It was not any easier for Andy Roddick when the teenager came up against Kroslak. After he eked out the first two sets, it looked as though this super-confident American would ease his way through, and when the third went into a tiebreak he was on the verge at 5–1. But Kroslak hung in, gathered an improbable momentum, and took six points in a row to extend the match to a fourth set. It needed another tiebreak to decide the outcome, but Roddick was determined not to make the same mistake twice and won it 7–1.

This meant that the Americans had only to win the doubles and the tie was theirs in two days. The team was untried, with James Blake partnering Fish in bright red shirts that matched the flashiness of their tennis. Mecir had no alternative but to throw Beck and Kroslak back into the fray and although, for the second day, they gave of their best and squeezed out a tiebreak set, it was not quite good enough. Fish could not believe how anything could be quite so uplifting.

"This ranks above anything else I've ever done," said the teenager. "The atmosphere is unlike anything else and though I've had a few good wins in my career, nothing comes close, not even close to this. Davis Cup is a different league."

Captain McEnroe was able to relish victory for the first time in the chair. And it was the first time in ten years that the Americans had won a doubles—they hadn't won since he was a player, with his brother John. "Let's just say I am glad to get the monkey off our back," said Patrick. "I'm not making any predictions or anything about the future, but obviously the way these guys played was a big statement. I want to see them keep improving. I am sure they will."

ABOVE: Pete Sampras returned to Davis Cup action with a four-set victory over Karol Beck.

OPPOSITE: James Blake and Mardy Fish sealed the United States' triumph in the doubles.

"I am going to get fired up for any Davis Cup I am playing— dead rubber, live rubber, 2-nothing, 0-2, **IT'S EXCITING.**"

JAMES BLAKE (U.S.A.)

CROATIA CELEBRATES
FIRST-EVER APPEARANCE
IN QUARTERFINALS

CROATIA V GERMANY

What more could the sport of tennis hold in store for the extraordinary Croat character Goran Ivanisevic? Goran had supposedly reached the summit in 2001, taking the Wimbledon title against every conceivable odd—the wild man with the wild card. His country cherished the moment he defeated Patrick Rafter. And when he bared his soul in his hometown of Split—having been flown home to a hero's welcome—they loved him even more.

But there was something else urging him on, something more that he wanted to do, something more for his country than just for him. Croatia was new to the Davis Cup, as it was new to so many other sports. It had first played in the competition in 1993, with its best performance to date a first round appearance in the World Group in 1995.

Ivanisevic held all the records, as one might have expected: Most Total Wins, Most Singles Wins, Most Doubles Wins, Most Ties Played, Most Years Played—and was half of the best Croatian doubles team with Sasa Hirszon. What he had not been able to do was inspire his country to a World Group victory and perhaps on to an opportunity to lift the precious cup itself.

The first round tie against Germany in Zagreb did not inspire much fear in the Croats. Indeed, their opponents were the ones with all the headaches. The Germans had a new captain, but he was confronted with the all-too-familiar problems. Michael Stich knew all about how to win at the highest level. The 1992 Wimbledon champion had won twenty-one of his thirty singles for his country in Davis Cup and been the mainstay of the 1993 championship winning side in Dusseldorf against Australia.

Those stunning experiences, however, were not protection from the uncertainty that still clouded the constitution of the German side. Stich knew what he was letting himself in for. For a start, there was little chance he would be able to select Tommy Haas in the foreseeable future.

Haas, who had reached the semifinals of the Australian Open in January, was still at loggerheads with the Deutscher Tennis Bund over what he described as "not paying enough attention to our players."

"They have promised a lot of things to us—and to me lately—and always at the last minute they take them away," he said. "At the beginning of the year, I had to make a point of view for my sake and say 'not with me anymore.'"

Stich would actually make a move in May to try to bring the parties closer together, but it remained to be seen when and where Haas might next represent his country.

With this bickering in the background, Stich knew the tie would be a burden and there was an intriguing subplot: Stich had been a member of the last German side to win the trophy, when Niki Pilic—now in charge of Croatia—was Germany's non-playing captain. Amid all the friendships, there was the serious business of winning to be addressed.

The Croats were on a high. Stich would have to rely on Nicolas Kiefer, now ranked well out of the

top ten but showing a greater desire for Davis Cup than he had in the past, and Rainer Schuettler, responding to the opportunity to reverse his 1–2 win-loss record in singles. Schuettler was drawn to face Ivan Ljubicic in the opening singles before Ivanisevic would be able to rouse the crowd to fever pitch.

Schuettler gave Stich the start he must have dreamed of. Despite losing the first set to Ljubicic, the twenty-five-year-old demonstrated wonderful powers of self-control and attacking verve, and performed as if he were at home, not in front of a full Croatian house. Schuettler won the second set on a tiebreak, swept the third, and though Ljubicic had three points to take the match into a fifth set, it was the German who prevailed to give his side an unexpected 1–0 lead.

As if there was not pressure enough on Ivanisevic, he now had to win his match against Kiefer simply to draw the sides level. The atmosphere was electric—akin to Centre Court at Wimbledon those seven months before—just the way Goran likes it.

You never really knew what was going on behind the composed façade of the German. Kiefer, as always, looked as though he hadn't a care in the world, and that he had just stepped out of a freezer onto the court. What Kiefer knew was that he had not beaten Ivanisevic in the past and that this time Goran was the most driven he had ever seen him.

At the start, it appeared that Ivanisevic was having more trouble with his shoulder and his contact lenses than with anything Kiefer could throw at him. Incredibly, the Croat had won the Wimbledon title with poor eyesight and he was using contact lenses for the first time. And he prevailed—brilliantly at times. "It was one of the best ever matches I have played in Davis Cup," said Ivanisevic after his 7–6, 6–3, 6–4 success.

Ivanisevic and Ljubicic had not been beaten in their three previous Davis Cup doubles, so the Germans, David Prinosil and Michael Kohlmann, knew they would have to be on a powerful wavelength to deny them. It was going to be a case of not squandering opportunities, but that is just what young Kohlmann did, making a hash of a straightforward overhead in the ninth game of the opening set. "Who knows what would have happened if we'd made that break," said Stich later. "It took all of the wind from my players."

Croatia, on the other hand, drew strength, winning the doubles in straight sets and providing Ivanisevic with the opportunity to have more glory heaped onto his shoulders. The left one still hurt him every time he raised a racket, but that was not going to be a handicap with a first World Group win in his nation's sights. Schuettler, who had shown courage on the first day, did not buckle in the intensity of the glare. He held on as best he could, dragging the Wimbledon champion into a couple of tiebreaks but this was to be another of Goran's days. His 6–4, 7–6, 7–6 win was his first in three meetings with Schuettler and his description of it as "one of the best of my career" was all but drowned out in the cacophonous Croat celebrations.

RUSSIA V SWITZERLAND

Roger Federer had been here before. In the first round of the 2001 World Group, the United States landed in Switzerland knowing one player was likely to stand in its path. Federer defeated both the American singles players, Todd Martin and Jan-Michael Gambill, and teamed up with Lorenzo Manta to win the doubles as well.

The result might just as well have read Federer 3, U.S.A. 2.

It was time for Federer to have another crack, this time against the Russians in Moscow but this time he would have some help. Michel Kratochvil, who had made his debut for the Swiss in the U.S. tie, now had a year's more experience and was more than capable of lending Federer a hand.

Even so, the task was a tall one. Ever since he had first spoken on the subject, Yevgeny Kafelnikov had made it clear that he had one overriding tennis ambition: to bring the Davis Cup by BNP Paribas to Russia by way of a tribute for all that the country had offered to him. This year, surely, was the final opportunity.

Kafelnikov had Marat Safin at his side, often a strength but sometimes not. Safin was in a permanent state of mercurial angst. Who knew, let alone his playing partner, if the younger man would be up for the Davis Cup, or would subside under the barrage of pressures the competition inevitably brings.

"It's a team competition, sometimes you play better, sometimes you play worse," was Safin's argument, one it was impossible with which to find fault. "We all suffer from nerves, this is not the same, this is Davis Cup. You are counting on other people and they are counting on you. And you don't want to lose at home."

Within an hour and thirty-six minutes of the tie against Switzerland starting, Safin was truly suffering. Federer came at him like a steam engine and would not relent. If the first set was tight, the second and third became a roll for the Swiss, so deep into despair did Safin sink. There was nothing Safin could do to raise himself out of his lethargy; Federer won 7–5, 6–1, 6–2. Part one of his Herculean effort had been completed.

OPPOSITE: Goran Ivanisevic celebrates his victory over Rainer Schuettler to secure Croatia's place in the quarterfinals.

ABOVE: Roger Federer (**LEFT**) gave Switzerland a great start in Moscow, before Michel Kratochvil (**RIGHT**) suffered a narrow five-set defeat by Yevgeny Kafelnikov.

ABOVE: Yevgeny Kafelnikov and Marat Safin kept Russia on track with a vital doubles win.

OPPOSITE: Roger Federer **(TOP LEFT)** defeated Kafelnikov to level the tie, before Marat Safin **(RIGHT)** saw Russia home to the delight of his playing partner **(BOTTOM LEFT).**

Enter Kratochvil and Kafelnikov. The match was to be one of the most pulsating of the first round, with the twenty-two-year-old from Bern coming back from a set down to lead by two sets to one. Kafelnikov—watched by former Russian President Boris Yeltsin, among others—managed to hang in the match, but when Kratochvil came out to serve at 6–5 in the fourth set, the impossible suddenly became a possibility.

"I knew I had the match right there but the game went so quickly, I didn't play defensively or afraid, I went for my shots but I just lost them," said the Swiss player.

True enough, he did not hold back but Kafelnikov survived to win the tiebreak and sweep an exhausted Kratochvil aside in the fifth set.

For the doubles, a crowd of 8,000 swelled into the Olympic Stadium and with their bench brandishing a huge Russian flag, the partnership of Kafelnikov and Safin was inspired to a 6–2, 7–6, 6–7, 6–2 victory over Federer and the veteran Marc Rosset (who was to become Safin's hitting partner and then Swiss Davis Cup captain later in the year).

It was up to Federer once more to sustain Switzerland through a third day. He did not let his country down, staying with Kafelnikov early on and then cruising through the gears, much as he had done against Safin on Friday. A 7–6, 6–1, 6–1 victory for Federer left his beaten opponent unable to explain away quite what caused his second and third set slump.

Safin, who had not yet come of age in Davis Cup, faced Kratochvil in the tie decider. Safin raced through the opening set but was gradually pegged back. The second set tiebreak was going to be crucial and, once Safin had found some glorious touches to win it 8–6, the Swiss knew they had nothing much left to give.

"I couldn't have given any more," said Federer on the back of Switzerland's 3-2 defeat. "It was tough that we lost the tie," he said, placing full emphasis on the word "we." The Russian captain, Shamil Tarpischev, knew his team had been erratic but that ultimately they had enough character to win through. It would stand them in excellent stead for the unfolding dramas ahead.

RUSSIA LEAVES IT LATE
BUT SURVIVES SWISS TEST

NOVAK INSPIRES CZECHS
TO VICTORY AGAINST BRAZIL

CZECH REPUBLIC V BRAZIL

There is no such thing as a one-man team—or so the theory goes—but when the Brazilians hitched up in smoky Ostrava for its first round meeting with the Czech Republic, they knew that the empty seat on the plane would take an awful lot of filling.

Gustavo Kuerten had been struggling with a hip injury for quite a few weeks and was now heading off to America for the consultation he hoped would mean a reasonably quick return to the tour. Unfortunately for Brazil this was akin to having the team's right arm severed, considering the twenty-five-year-old had played fourteen consecutive ties for his country during which time they had reached a semifinal and two quarterfinals.

Not only that, but Kuerten's long-time doubles partner Jaime Oncins had announced during 2001 that he would be retiring at the end of the year, giving due notice of his intent. What is more, the Czechs had hardly rolled out the red carpet. To be more precise, it was a lightning-fast green one.

The Brazilians fielded Fernando Meligeni and debutant Andre Sa as their singles players. Sa was thrust into the pressure cooker straight away in the first singles against Jiri Novak, who had returned to his homeland having reached the semifinals of the Australian Open at the end of January.

Sa's initial response to an extreme task was to shock the Czechs out of any feelings of complacency they may have had once Kuerten's absence was confirmed. Novak was hesitant, inevitably so with so much riding on his performance, and Sa noted it. The first set tiebreak was won 12–10 by the Brazilian, who saved two set points en route. "I knew he was playing with nothing to lose, which made him a very dangerous opponent," said Novak. "Yet even though I lost that first set I still felt inside that I was in control. I had to keep my focus and I felt I would win."

Novak was true to his inner feelings, sweeping through the next two sets comfortably. Though he suffered an early break in the fourth, he treated it as a minor inconvenience, taking the match 6–7, 6–1, 6–1, 6–4. From that moment on, the Czechs were imperious.

The powerful serving and sustained aggression of Bohdan Ulihrach was too much for Meligeni. His straight sets victory was sufficient for Novak and David Rikl—one of the most formidable doubles teams in the world—to play with great freedom on what is normally the most fraught occasion of the weekend. Sa and Alexandre Simoni were, by comparison, lambs to the slaughter. Never had the beaches of Rio seemed quite so far away.

Though the Brazilian pair built up a 4–1 lead, they were spun around as the Czechs took five games in a row. There were signs of a possible revival in the third set when Simoni and Sa came back from 4–1 down to level at 5–5, but the Czechs stepped up the pace a touch and were through to the quarterfinals in two days.

"It is not always easy to be the favorites and in Davis Cup you cannot underestimate anyone," said the canny Czech captain, Jan Kukal. "I must admit, though, that my players did what I expected them to do."

OPPOSITE: Jiri Novak **(LEFT)** and Bohdan Ulihrach **(BOTTOM RIGHT)** led the Czech Republic to victory over a weakened Brazilian team led by Fernando Meligeni **(TOP RIGHT)**.

ABOVE: Andre Sa made a bright start against Novak before losing the opening rubber in four sets.

PROFILE: GORAN IVANISEVIC

BORN | SEPTEMBER 13, 1971, IN SPLIT, CROATIA
TURNED PROFESSIONAL | 1988
DAVIS CUP RECORDS | SINGLES 28–9 | DOUBLES 19–6

D O YOU REMEMBER THE PICTURE TAKEN at the end of the 2000 Wimbledon Champions' Parade when fifty-seven of the figures who blessed twentieth-century Wimbledon were captured for all time? The man at the extreme left of the back row looked as if he'd rather have been somewhere else. His smile was forced, his demeanor morose. It had taken every bit of persuasion his friends knew to get Goran Ivanisevic out there at all.

The court on which Ivanisevic trod that magical Saturday afternoon conjured so many negative emotions. Three times a Wimbledon runner-up, he went through the motions and hoped it would end sooner rather than later. What a difference it would make if they could digitally remaster the picture, painting out the 2000 Goran image to replace it with the face of Goran 2001.

He has barely stopped smiling since, although a dreadful shoulder injury, which meant he could not sustain Croatia's challenge beyond the quarterfinals of the 2002 Davis Cup, has led him to reassess how much further he might go in his tennis career. The sport misses him.

That Ivanisevic is a one-off goes without saying, even though he suggested during that magical Wimbledon that there are, in fact, three Gorans: the happy one, the angry one, and the one he calls in an emergency to separate like from dislike. He is a man of moods, of moments of sheer fun and exasperation.

"Nothing is normal with Goran, which is why we all love him," said his manager, Gerard Tsobanian. "There is no more generous person in the world, no one who thinks more of others. He worships his friends and his family; the group around him never changes. Many people had lost faith in Goran but they never did. I remember before he won Wimbledon, I tried to get commercial deals for him in the past two years, but people said 'Oh hasn't he retired yet?' Now, they have stopped laughing and saying 'Sorry, next player please.' Now they have to listen to me again."

But he could always take up soccer. He has always wanted to be a center forward for his favorite team, Dynamo Zagreb. On a wild Tuesday last October, he got his wish in front of a crowd of forty thousand to say farewell to one of Croatia's greatest stars, Zvonimir Boban. Although the home side lost 2–1, Ivanisevic came on as a substitute for Boban, wearing his famous number 10 shirt, before scoring Croatia's only goal. It was, he said, almost as proud a moment as winning Wimbledon itself.

He had a spell in the army for Croatia, where national service is still considered a vital component of a man's makeup. Whether he was best suited to the discipline is another matter. How fondly one recalls an incident at Brighton in 2000, when Ivanisevic smashed yet another in a long line of rackets that had splintered while under his spell. He dug into his bag for another, only to find he had used them all. There was no other choice for the referee but to disqualify him. One laughed both with him and at him that night. Never again.

FRANCE d. CZECH REPUBLIC 3–2 | Pau, France • indoor carpet
USA d. SPAIN 3–1 | Houston, Tx, USA • outdoor grass
RUSSIA d. SWEDEN 4–1 | Moscow, Russia • indoor clay
ARGENTINA d. CROATIA 3–2 | Buenos Aires, Argentina • outdoor clay

SAMPRAS STUMBLES
BUT USA ADVANCES
TO SEMIFINALS

USA V SPAIN

The Westside Club, in an affluent stretch of Houston, Texas, has spent a small fortune preparing for and marketing itself as the four Grand Slam tennis championships rolled into one.

The well-heeled members are treated to splendid surroundings unlike any across the rest of the world. If they want to spend a day being Rene Lacoste or Gustavo Kuerten, there is red clay from Roland Garros. Or they can pretend to be Chris Evert or Andre Agassi, pounding away on the Decoturf of Flushing Meadows.

The Rebound Ace courts that directly ape Rod Laver Arena in Melbourne Park give the club a taste of Aussie-land. But they have grass courts too. When the first round matches in the Davis Cup by BNP Paribas were completed, the club determined that it should stage the tie against Spain and came up with the perfect argument to back up its case.

The club's prominent owners, Linda and Jim McIngvale, had wanted to make certain they planted the very best grass. Linda admitted: "At first nobody seemed to know what they were talking about when grass was mentioned. But Dennis Ralston and Roscoe Tanner, who live in the area, both said that Queen's Club in London had the finest grass courts anywhere in the world.

"We contacted Queen's and asked if we could borrow their head groundsman Dave Kimpton for a while so that he could help us out. Dave came across and looked at what we had. He said the Bermuda grass was okay, but there wasn't a soil here that would duplicate Queen's—and that was the secret to producing a perfect grass court."

Never a couple to be beaten, the McIngvales decided to import thirty-two containers of soil from England, even though the local Texan customs and excise argued that they couldn't possibly allow so much foreign "dirt" into the States. But customs was aware that they were dealing with a man who thrived under the pseudonym "Mattress Mac"—his bedding and furniture business was one of the most famous chains in Houston. He did not back down.

Finally, after stretching the argument back and forth, the customs office relented and, with Kimpton's careful nurturing, the McIngvales were delivered the grass they so cherished. With this and the rekindling of Pete Sampras's love affair with the Davis Cup in mind, Houston seemed the perfect venue for U.S.A. v. Spain. The Spaniards had a noted dislike—almost hatred—of grass, and the Davis Cup was about wringing every last little advantage possible from a home draw.

It did not take long for the USTA to agree that Sampras, Andy Roddick, Todd Martin, James Blake, and Houston were a perfect fit. The Spanish, who had enticed the Americans to Santander in the 2000 semifinals—providing one of the slowest clay courts ever—could hardly have been surprised to be confronted with something as alien as grass.

"We understand but we cannot just change our game in three or four days," said Spain's most experienced player, Alex Corretja. "We have made some adjustments and we will have to see if they are enough for us to win."

When Jim Courier, twice the champion of Roland Garros and now coach to the U.S. team, had talked of making Spain feel as uncomfortable as possible, Corretja knew exactly what he had in mind. "It's weird for us because we're just not used to it," he said. "But in one day, anything can happen— no matter what the surface—and we strongly believe we have chances to win."

Corretja, the mainstay of Spain, would have to wait until the second singles to see if his "adjustments" had any effect. He would face Sampras—seven times a Wimbledon singles champion and the overwhelming favorite—even if this was to be his very first match on grass on U.S. "soil," so to speak.

OPPOSITE: Pete Sampras **(TOP LEFT)** suffered a shock five-set defeat by Alex Corretja **(BOTTOM LEFT)**, but fellow American James Blake **(RIGHT)** was left jumping for joy after his doubles victory.

The first match would pit Roddick and Tommy Robredo, the two shining prospects of their respective countries—and adversaries since their junior days. Robredo, six months the older, had not played a Davis Cup tie before and could hardly have chosen a more arduous task. "For me it is a dream to start the battle, and every day I think my game on the grass is improving," he said.

The most conspicuous memory of the match was how many errors littered it, probably caused by the nerves of both players. Roddick had started a Davis Cup tie before at home, but not one of this prestige. Robredo was in at the deep end and it took him a long time to shake off the nerves. In total, there were 103 unforced errors in three sets, fifty-three of them committed by the Spaniard. The mistakes, however, merely contrived to add a certain edge to a match that already had plenty riding on it.

Roddick proved, as he had done before, to be slightly Robredo's superior, especially when the bigger points were concerned. His 6–3, 7–5, 7–6 (9–7) victory sent the locals wild because there was an unbridled sense of optimism that with Sampras next up against Corretja, the U.S.A. would head into Friday night with a comfortable cushion. No one in the Texas gambling rooms—nor anywhere else for that matter—would have bet a red cent on the Spaniard.

One remembered Corretja's words—"in one day anything can happen"—but not this day, surely. Although Sampras didn't exactly roll the first two sets and was occasionally troubled when the rallies were extended, he seemed well on the way. What followed was a turnaround that sent shock waves across the tennis world.

It was difficult to tell whether Sampras started cruising or Corretja picked up his game a notch or two. The American had been dominant without being overpowering, but in the third set, Corretja would not be swept aside. He hung into the rallies, drawing errors from Sampras, and the body language told him that he had a chance if he could stick around.

Perhaps on more than any other surface, a tiebreak on grass is a crap-shoot. "You roll the dice a little bit," said Sampras, "and they came down on his side." To lose one set was considered careless; to drop the next two as well was little short of extraordinary. "I felt I had my chances but I kept letting them slip," said Sampras. "Even though I've been so successful on grass, it can still take time to get your confidence. Alex began to win the break points, it can happen."

A match that ninety-nine times out of one hundred Sampras would sweep through, he lost in worrying circumstances. Corretja and the Spanish team embraced in the middle of a court that had been tailor-made for this man to commiserate with his teammates. "I'm kicking myself a little bit," said Sampras, "I had a ton of chances, I really did. Grass is a crazy surface sometimes but I've still done pretty OK on it over the years."

At the height of their celebration, though, there had to be some concern that the match had taken so much from Corretja's tank that he would not be able to raise himself for the doubles or, more importantly, for a reverse singles.

The announcement of captain Jordi Arrese's line-up the next morning confirmed Spain's worst fears. Not only was Corretja out on his feet, he had injured the thumb of his racquet hand and could not grip it properly. So Arrese brought in Alberto Martin, another Davis Cup debutant. With an unfamiliar partner, Juan Balcells was unable to reproduce the magic he had brought to previous doubles episodes with Corretja and, in a rain-interrupted match, Todd Martin and James Blake had very little trouble securing a 6–1, 6–4, 6–4 victory.

"I don't think any doubles match I've played in my life has meant as much to me as my two doubles in the Davis Cup," said Blake. "This is really something cool."

Andy Roddick, growing with experience with each match, had already learned when to press his advantage. With Corretja still recuperating from Friday's heroics, the Spaniards decided to throw Martin to the wolf who wore a sun visor on a cloudy day. Roddick was not to be denied, sweeping to victory in straight sets, 6–2, 6–4, 6–2 with a performance of near flawless tennis. His reaction at the end was to stride, one arm raised, into his captain's embrace before grabbing the flag and parading it around the court—showing just how much the victory meant to the young American.

"I freak out a little bit during Davis Cup," he said. "It's just the emotion of playing for your country, the crowd going nuts and just, you know, playing for your teammates. It's a rush."

Roddick had now extended his unbeaten record in the competition to 7–0, the best start by an American in the competition since Agassi made his debut in 1988. There was clearly a whole lot more to come.

Andy Roddick's **(LEFT)** victories over Tommy Robredo **(SECOND LEFT)** and Alberto Martin disappointed the Spanish supporters **(SECOND RIGHT)**, but earned the congratulations of U.S. captain Patrick McEnroe **(RIGHT)**.

FRANCE OVERCOMES
CZECH CHALLENGE
TO REACH LAST FOUR

FRANCE V CZECH REPUBLIC

When the name Cedric Pioline was omitted from the French squad by captain Guy Forget to take on the Czech Republic in Pau, the assumption was that it signaled the end of a stalwart eight-year story in the competition.

Pioline could hardly have believed he would add a second Davis Cup winner's medal in 2001 to the one he garnered in Malmo in 1995, but his stirring contribution was as vital as anyone's in Melbourne. The doubles victory with Fabrice Santoro over Patrick Rafter and Lleyton Hewitt helped create the levels of tension that would ultimately seal France's victory.

Four months later and the old bones were creaking just that little bit more than Forget could place his faith in. Michael Llodra was preferred in the doubles with Santoro, a left-right combination that was to prove irresistible. Forget did not go on record as indicating this was the end for Pioline, but the sages sensed it would take something pretty miraculous for the thirty-two-year-old to win his place back.

The younger guard marched forward: Sebastien Grosjean was regarded among the finest players in the world; Nicolas Escude had moments of magic; Santoro could still confound anyone on his day. And the tall, lean Llodra—a hitting partner in Melbourne—had begun to show such signs of steady improvement that he could no longer be held back.

The Czech captain Jan Kukal had no such luxuries. His team was more or less chosen for him, yet it was one with much going for it. Jiri Novak had reached the semifinals of the Australian Open and looked to be heading for his best-ever year on the Tour. His partnership with David Rikl was among the most formidable in doubles and Bohdan Ulihrach had long shown contempt for the form book.

The tie was tantalizingly poised, but home advantage was thought likely to play to France's favor, since Pau was regarded as something of a lucky venue. France had played there three times and won on each occasion, against Yugoslavia in 1991 and both Belgium and Brazil in 1999. The surface was going to be slick.

Grosjean had a point to prove, which made him more dangerous than before. He had been beaten in both singles in the 2001 final, by Rafter on the opening day, and Hewitt on the third, before Australia's hopes were dashed by Escude in the final, scintillating rubber.

It is not as if Grosjean did not feel worthy of his place in the ensuing parades. It was just a little difficult for someone of his talent to have to swallow two such direct hits. And so there was something driving him on more than the simple desire to win. He had helped France to their first round victory over Holland, but he wanted to make sure they returned to the final, and that he was the man at the forefront of that particular procession.

Grosjean would meet Ulihrach in the first rubber. The Frenchman was still troubled by a problem in his left abductor that caused him to pull up every now and again. Ulihrach was a player whose form could rise and fall in a single rally, let alone the course of a match, making tactics against him difficult to establish.

It turned into a tense match. Grosjean took the first set, but then lost his service action completely, so that Ulihrach began confidently nailing his returns, and sweeping a succession of passing shots out of the Frenchman's reach. From 3–3 in the second set, Ulihrach ran off nine games in a row, looking like a massive upset was on the card.

"I tried to make him play, hoping he would make mistakes," Grosjean admitted afterwards but it was he who was in serious trouble. Captain Guy Forget was getting into a state in the chair, but nothing he said could spark a response.

OPPOSITE: Jiri Novak's **(BOTTOM LEFT)** wins over Nicolas Escude and Sebastien Grosjean **(TOP LEFT)** were in vain for the Czech Republic, after Fabrice Santoro **(RIGHT)** defeated Bohdan Ulihrach in the deciding rubber in Pau.

ABOVE: Ulihrach suffered the agony of five-set defeats by both Grosjean and Santoro.

But with his nose in front to some extent, Ulihrach could not bring himself to go for the kill. His serve suddenly buckled, to the extent that he won only three of his last eight service games of the match. Meanwhile, Grosjean steadied his own serve and nerve (as well as the 7,000 crowd in the Palais des Sports) to race away with the rubber 6–3, 3–6, 0–6, 6–3, 6–1 in two hours and fifty-seven minutes.

The French knew that whereas Ulihrach was likely to have moments of distraction in which he was vulnerable, Novak rightly enjoyed a reputation for resolutely steady tennis, never more so than in his current mood. He was at No. 6 in the ATP Champions Race heading into the tie, thanks in no small measure to his semifinal appearance at the Australian Open where he lost in five titanic sets to Thomas Johansson.

His opponent Escude had excelled himself on the tour between missing out on the first round tie and being chosen to spearhead the French challenge in the quarters. He had, in order of events, reached the semifinals in Milan, the final in Marseille, and won the title in Rotterdam on a surface very similar to that in Pau. But Novak was steadiness personified, taking the first set on a tiebreak and racing through the second 6–1 in a twenty-minute onslaught, subjecting Escude to a barrage of deep returns and lacerating passing shots.

The response from the crowd was to lift Escude in the third set—and it looked like he would be inspired to one of his five-set comebacks. However, Novak held himself together, winning in four sets to render Escude's first defeat in singles in the Cup.

After the rise came the incredible fall. What shocked those at courtside for the doubles between Novak and Rikl and the new pairing of Santoro and Llodra was how little the Czechs spoke to each other. Though the French twosome made few errors, the Czechs seemed to surrender much too easily, losing in straight sets with barely a whimper.

And so, whereas he had been so quiet on Saturday, Novak was rejuvenated the next afternoon, sweeping past an increasingly immobile Grosjean in four sets. Despite a start similar to the one he had made against Ulihrach, the French No. 1 was stymied by Novak's resourcefulness, and a tweaked hamstring in the third set did not help his cause. The tie was poised at 2-2 with big decisions to be made.

Escude had a 0–3 head-to-head rating against Ulihrach, and had done some damage to his left knee against Novak on Friday. The French team doctor said that Escude was "basically OK" but it would be a risk to play him.

Forget asked Santoro "Are you ready to play?" to which he got an unreserved "Yes." The decision had to be made by the French captain, and he went with Santoro, a choice that seemed to have been utterly vindicated when he led Ulihrach by two sets to love, with the crowd ready to celebrate a tumultuous victory.

Nothing in Davis Cup comes easily, though. Santoro had expended a ton of energy in those two sets and Ulihrach began to take risks, hitting the ball as deep and as near to the lines as he dared. The strategy began to pay dividends.

Forget tried to speak to Santoro at changeovers, but felt nothing was getting through, so he decided to get angry. "Start to be aggressive, start to do something, or we are going to the wall," he said.

From somewhere, as the tie entered the fifth set of the fifth rubber, Santoro found the will to fight again. Serving at 3–3, Ulihrach made a couple of errors to hand Santoro the priceless break. As the Czech player's limbs began to cramp, so his shots began to miss the lines. After four hours and fifteen minutes, Santoro and all of France celebrated a 7–6, 7–5, 3–6, 4–6, 6–3 victory that was his first in a decisive fifth rubber since making his debut as a teenager against Australia eleven years before.

"Bohdan was fighting unbelievably, but I just had enough in the end," Santoro said. "I am very, very proud."

ARGENTINA V CROATIA

Goran Ivanisevic was visibly distraught. He had retired from his opening match at Key Biscayne—against Franco Squillari of Argentina after seven games—before striding into the pressroom to be confronted with two journalists. For the Wimbledon champion, that situation alone was a kick in the teeth; as for the news he had to impart, he deserved a bigger audience, one in which compassion would have been more widespread.

"I made my dream last year," Ivanisevic said. "If somebody told me before Wimbledon last year that I would never play tennis again, I'd pick Wimbledon. Maybe God heard me that day and said: 'OK, Goran, this is enough for you.' The rotator cuff is getting bigger and my arm is killing me. As soon as I hit the big serve, I can't hit the second shot. The doctor said it can be a lottery, one week good and then three weeks, really bad."

The Croatian captain Niki Pilic hoped that seven days in Buenos Aires might just turn out to be one of those "good" weeks. But he was also deeply concerned that Ivanisevic could not possibly last such a test—on slow clay, playing against one of the most formidable teams in the world.

"They will be dumping the clay at least six inches deep and watering it a lot," said Ivanisevic in Florida. He held out little hope of being able to play a lasting part in what had started as a year filled with optimism for Croatian tennis. "I just don't see how I can possibly play three matches in three days. The shoulder won't be able to stand it."

There was a strong suggestion that Ivanisevic might fly to Split rather than suffer the agony of watching Croatia in what was being touted, in his anticipated absence, as a possible rout in Argentina's favor. Ironically, Squillari, who had profited from Ivanisevic's withdrawal in Florida, was not considered for the squad. Captain Alejandro Gattiker had plumped for a youthful side, built around the prolific talents of Gaston Gaudio and Juan Ignacio Chela.

Coming into the tie, Gaudio had amassed a 7–0 singles record in Davis Cup, five before the 2002 championship and two more in the first-round defeat of John Fitzgerald's Australia. But Chela was the higher ranked, and so would face the Croatian number 2, Ivo Karlovic, on the opening day, leaving Gaudio to open proceedings against the lugubrious but highly talented Ivan Ljubicic.

OPPOSITE: Fabrice Santoro celebrates France's passage to the semifinals.

ABOVE: Gaston Gaudio **(LEFT)** extended his unbeaten Davis Cup run in singles to nine matches in front of a packed stadium **(RIGHT)** in Buenos Aires.

ARGENTINA SURVIVES
CROATIAN COMEBACK
TO REACH SEMIFINALS

"At this moment, in this place, on this surface, Gaudio is better than me," said Ljubicic in what would prove to be an honest assessment of the outcome of that first match. Though he was able to stay with the twenty-three-year-old in the opening set that went to a tiebreak, Ljubicic's words were to have a prophetic ring: Gaudio stormed through the second and third for a 7–6, 6–2, 6–3 victory.

Precious little was known of Karlovic, who did not even merit a mention in the annual media guide to the players. He had won a place in the side after Pilic arranged a five-set play-off against Zelko Krajan, the prize for which was a Davis Cup berth. The difference that day was Karlovic's huge serve.

A much bigger test awaited him—a match against Juan Ignacio Chela, back playing tennis again after six months spent on the sidelines, having been banned after a positive drug test. The Karlovic serve was in pretty good fettle in the opening set, when he stunned Chela—ranked 160 places above him—and probably himself by clinching it 7–5. It did seem, though, as if it was only a matter of time before Chela's greater all-court talents would take the steam out of the Croat and the match began to take a more predictable course from the middle of the second set.

The new boy acquitted himself brilliantly, but Chela prevailed 5–7, 6–4, 6–4, 6–2, to leave the Argentines on the threshold of a place in the last four. Enter big Goran. There was really no way that Ivanisevic should have been out there at all, but nothing mattered more to him than trying to inspire the country that worshipped him to the Davis Cup semifinals. The tennis that afternoon was to reach peaks he had not previously touched since that glorious Wimbledon summer of 2001.

Caught in the whirlwind were Lucas Arnold and Guillermo Canas, who should have been out partying early when they won the first two sets. Appropriately, a flow of dark clouds scuttled across the court as Ivanisevic and Ljubicic began to find their range, each lifting the other in turn. A storm sent the players running for cover, with the Croat team leading in the third set. They provoked a second thunderbolt when they raced through the fourth set 6–0. Arnold and Canas settled a little in the fifth and had a match point at 5–4, only to have it swept aside by another bludgeoning stroke from Ivanisevic. Three games later, the Croats snatched the break themselves and stood firm for one of the most remarkable victories seen in Davis Cup, 4–6, 2–6, 6–3, 6–0, 8–6.

"We had heard before the match that Argentina had not lost a doubles at home in thirteen years," Ljubicic said. "We wanted to be the ones who broke that record. It was a magnificent win. Goran started serving really well in the third set and that gave us the impetus. With the kind of crowd they had, you have to fight."

Ivanisevic admitted that it was a hell-for-leather decision to play. "I had problems for one and a half sets, but it (the shoulder) started to feel a little better and I found a decent level and motion, which made it hurt less," he said. "I knew my shoulder would not survive having to serve every second game in the singles. We have given ourselves a chance. They have to win, we can go out and try to enjoy it."

Ljubicic took his teammate at his word. Against Chela in the first reverse singles, he started defiantly, winning the first set and, despite a collapse in the second, he roused himself to an

OPPOSITE: Goran Ivanisevic and Ivan Ljubicic (TOP RIGHT) pulled off an astonishing doubles victory, but Juan Ignacio Chela (LEFT) and Gaston Gaudio (BOTTOM RIGHT) steered Argentina into the Davis Cup semifinals.

ABOVE: The Croatian fans were in fine voice in Buenos Aires.

astonishing level in the third and fourth, to win 6–3, 1–6, 7–6, 6–4. He described it as his best-ever
performance on clay—anywhere—saying: "I really enjoyed the crowd's participation. The atmosphere
was fantastic and the reception I received from them as I left the court was something I'll never forget."

What Croatia would not have given to have had Ivanisevic out there for the fifth match, but both he
and they knew it was impossible. What was the point of jeopardizing what was left of a wonderful
career, for one match? And what if Karlovic could rise above and give Croatia a place in the semifinals?
It would give Ivanisevic something to aim for in the fall.

Of course, it was too much to hope for. Karlovic stood his ground against Gaudio for as long as his
lack of experience would allow, but once the Argentine got on a roll, he was unstoppable. A straight sets
victory—under the watchful eye of Diego Maradona, Argentina's greatest-ever soccer player—was
greeted with dancing in the streets. "This is the happiest moment of my life, nothing compares to it,"
Gaudio said. "My game went off for a while; it was not easy to play knowing that Maradona was
watching. He was always my idol. But it lasted for a few minutes and I came back strongly. It is a day
I will never forget."

Argentina had reached the semifinals for the first time in twenty-one years and their captain,
Alejandro Gattiker, was having difficulty keeping his emotions in check. "We knew it would be tough, all
the way through," he said. "Ivanisevic, Ljubicic, these are brilliant players. After the doubles, the whole
team went to sleep early because we knew what the final day would bring. At 2–2, Gaudio came out
and played at a very good level. I told him, this would be different, more than he had ever been used to,
but he responded superbly. I have so many competitive players to choose from, I am fortunate to be the
captain at such a wonderful time for tennis in Argentina."

True, Gattiker had Gaudio, Chela, and Canas in the front line. And then there was David Nalbandian,
a twenty-year-old of Armenian stock, who was forcing his way up the rankings. As the year progressed,
who would have had the audacity to think that, a year after Centre Court and the Wimbledon final, this
most famous son of Croatia would be replaced by an Argentinian that few of us had ever heard of?
The year was about to play more tricks on us.

"THIS IS THE DAY I WILL NEVER FORGET: getting Argentina to the Davis Cup semifinal, and having Maradona watch my match."
GASTON GAUDIO (ARG)

RUSSIA ENDS SWEDISH JINX
TO KEEP DREAM ALIVE

RUSSIA V SWEDEN

Sweden's captain Carl-Axel Hageskog had already announced that he was nearing the end of his tenure with the team. He had a superb run, but it was soon to be someone else's turn.

What better send off could there have been for one of the nicest men in the sport than to win the Davis Cup for the third time as captain? The Swedes' victory over Great Britain in Birmingham had been gloriously won, with Hageskog's decision to use Thomas Johansson as a "wild card" selection proving to be a masterstroke of captaincy.

Against the Russians in the 14,000-seater Luzhniki Sports Palace, upon a clay court that had been laid as a temporary surface, the Swedes' selection was much more straightforward. The Swedes, contrary to opinion, were not the masters of clay. Enqvist had been defeated in the first round at Roland Garros in his first four appearances there, while Johansson had never needed to extend his hotel reservation beyond the first couple of days.

The Russians had thrived on the surface, with Yevgeny Kafelnikov winning the French title in 1996, along with one semifinal and three quarterfinal appearances. Marat Safin had exploded onto the international scene at Roland Garros in 1998 and had spent his formative years in Spain, under the stewardship of Rafael Mensua. He was as well adjusted on clay as any player in the world.

The Swedes would have loved to have been able to bring Magnus Norman into their team but the 2000 Roland Garros runner-up was still struggling for full fitness after hip surgery. Enqvist and Johansson it had to be, but Hageskog knew that his men had won through difficult moments before, and they would not be intimidated by the task.

"I have a lot of faith in my players," he said. "We know it is going to be a tough task because the Russians are a very strong team, but we thrive when people don't expect us to do so well. We had to come from 2–1 down in the tie against Great Britain. The Swedish mentality is as good as it ever was. The Davis Cup is something that is very dear to us."

The tie was a repeat of the 2001 quarterfinal, when Sweden took advantage of Safin's absence through injury to defeat Russia 4–1. The tables were turned a year later, as Russia sought to end a four-match losing streak against the seven-time champions.

The first rubber was to be a rerun of the Australian Open final only two months earlier, Johansson versus Safin. The result in Melbourne had been totally at odds with most predictions but took small account of the improved game and the burning desire of Johansson to emerge from the shadows of Borg, Edberg, and Wilander. "I want to win so badly that sometimes I get tight," said the Swede, who, unlike so many of his sporting ancestors, does not try to hide the intensity of his fighting spirit. Indeed one would have a hard time recognizing Johansson as a typical Swedish sportsman.

OPPOSITE: Thomas Johansson **(TOP LEFT)** and Thomas Enqvist **(BOTTOM LEFT)** were left floundering as Yevgeny Kafelnikov and Marat Safin **(RIGHT)** completed victory over Sweden in two days.

"Right after Melbourne I was so relaxed," he said. "I beat Greg (Rusedski) in the first round tie in Birmingham and I was the kind of guy I would love to be every day. It is something I have been working on with my coach, not laying so much on the line all the time. I need to try to tell myself that it can be fun on the court as well.

"I like the attitude of someone like (Jiri) Novak. You cannot tell from his face after a match if he has lost or won. I worked like that for a while, but then the old Thomas came back. I am really competitive and intense."

He would need to be all of that in the Safin rematch and yet Johansson started as if his legs were set in concrete. It can happen in Davis Cup, where a player becomes overcome with tension, so much so that it is terribly hard to move in the direction he wants. Johansson was 4–0 down before he had laid a definitive racket on the ball. Safin, on the contrary, was serving out of his socks, and was able to maintain his percentages all the way through the three sets required. Safin won 6–4, 6–4, 6–4, a victory played to loud acclaim that would require the Swedes to sow every bit of the determination that had been the bedrock of their Davis Cup successes.

But this was the moment, too, for Yevgeny Kafelnikov to have a major say. The win over Michel Kratochvil in the opening round aside, it had been a relatively unforgettable start to the year for the twenty-eight year old. His best performance of the year to date had been reaching the semifinals in Marseille, where he lost in three tight sets to Thomas Enqvist.

That was reason enough for Kafelnikov to want to turn the screw on the Swedes, one that doubled in significance when Enqvist appeared on the opposite side of the net. The first set turned out to be crucial, with Enqvist picking up where he left off against Henman and Rusedski, staying with the Russian into the tiebreak, in which he led 5–3. If he could have driven on from here, Sweden would have had a terrific chance, but Kafelnikov was undaunted. He picked up his own game a notch or two, clawing back the mini-break and taking the set 8–6 in the breaker. It was all the impetus the Russian needed to move on, losing only four games in the following two sets.

It was all or nothing for Sweden now, and at least in Johansson and Jonas Bjorkman, they had a pair that, if it lacked for a track record together, was blessed with talent and tenacity. Bjorkman was one of the finest doubles players in the world—he had been rejuvenated in singles as well—and helped Johansson steer Sweden into a 6–3, 4–2 lead. The fightback had well and truly begun.

Safin and Kafelnikov exchanged sharp words. They did not want to have to come back on Sunday against Sweden with their tails up, so their focus and attitude hardened still further.

When the second set entered a tiebreak, it was, once again, a matter of a moment of inspiration, with Safin engineering the critical mini-break with a couple of audacious interceptions. Although they squandered a 3–1 lead to lose the third set on another breaker, the Russians regrouped, breaking Bjorkman's serve to take a wonderful fourth set 7–5, before holding their nerve to win 3–6, 7–6, 6–7, 7–5, 6–3 in three-and-a-half hours. The tie was theirs.

"I have achieved most of my goals in tennis, grand slam titles, an Olympic gold medal, becoming world number 1," Kafelnikov said. "The one thing left to give me full satisfaction is to win the Davis Cup. I should retire a happy man if that happened. People think I'm joking but I'm not. The tennis fans in Russia should come and watch the semifinal against Argentina as there will be fewer chances of seeing me play at home."

"We have our best chance, there is no doubt of that. Marat is coming of age as a Davis Cup player, we have an extremely good relationship and he wants to do something for the Russian people. This is definitely our chance."

Sweden would have to regroup, but it would be without Hageskog at the helm, replaced by Mats Wilander in the autumn. "I have a feeling like a very good dinner," Hageskog said at the conclusion of his eighth year in charge. "There is still a little bit left on the plate, but I am satisfied."

Russia's two-man team of Marat Safin (RIGHT) and Yevgeny Kafelnikov (LEFT) scored singles victories over Thomas Johansson and Thomas Enqvist (SECOND LEFT) before outlasting Jonas Bjorkman and Johansson (SECOND RIGHT) in a five-set doubles thriller.

PROFILE: ANDY RODDICK

BORN | AUGUST 30, 1982, IN OMAHA, NEBRASKA, UNITED STATES
TURNED PROFESSIONAL | 2000
DAVIS CUP RECORDS | SINGLES 7–2| DOUBLES 0-0

He hates to lose," says the American Davis Cup captain, Patrick McEnroe. "You think of (Jimmy) Connors and the way he competed on every single point. Andy's like that. He enjoys the moment, being in a big fight. To him, tennis is 'let's get it on.'" With an endorsement like that, how can Roddick go wrong? He is a massive hit with the females, a strapping six feet two inches, which means that he towers over most players in the world, and could pass for a rock star. Indeed, if he wasn't a tennis player, that is what he might have become.

There is no doubt that Andy Roddick would be big at something, but he clicked at tennis from an early age. When he got a little too big for Omaha, Nebraska, his family moved first to Texas and then to Florida, ostensibly to help sate his older brother John's desire to play tennis. But it was Andy's game that took off. Just before he played the under-18 U.S. championships in Michigan three years ago, he teamed up with Algerian-born player-turned-coach Tarik Benhabiles, a partnership that thrives still.

His distinguishing feature, looks aside, is his serve—one of the most intimidating the men's game has seen. He backs that up with what McEnroe describes as the best second serve around, mixing a three-quarter pace effort with a kicker of Pat Rafter-like consequence.

His forehand is just as formidable, a combination of pace and paint-the-lines accuracy. "I still have a lot of work to do," Roddick says about himself. "I was kind of thrown to the wolves in 2001 with the game I had but I've been able to work on things and to learn what I need to work on by mixing it with the top players. I don't think there's one shot of mine that's there— that's where I want it to be. But competition is what it is all about. If my brother tells me he can run to the gas station faster, I want to start off sprinting."

Put Roddick out on a tennis court and he is transformed from the easy-going Andy into the hyper-competitive A-Rod, who plays each point as if it is his last. Those present on Court Philippe Chatrier at Roland Garros a couple of years ago could never forget the moment he cramped against Michael Chang and staggered across the court. His bravery was remarkable and he only lost the final set 7–5 against the master marathon player.

He also has a happy knack of doing the right things off the court. At the Davis Cup tie against Spain in April, he lobbied the United States Tennis Association to set up a kids' clinic in Houston (a first, according to Davis Cup publicity staff). And, after clinching the tie for his country, he volunteered for an autograph session that lasted well over an hour.

He knows most of the neighbors who surround his home in Boca Raton. He has knocked on most of their doors to tell them to let him know if the music he plays is too loud. He often orders an extra pizza for the security guard when he orders one for himself. Quite a kid. "Tennis has already brought me quite a lot of cool things," he says. "I'm out here having a wicked time."

FRANCE d. USA 3–2 | Paris, France • outdoor clay
RUSSIA d. ARGENTINA 3–2 | Moscow, Russia • indoor carpet

SEMIFINALS

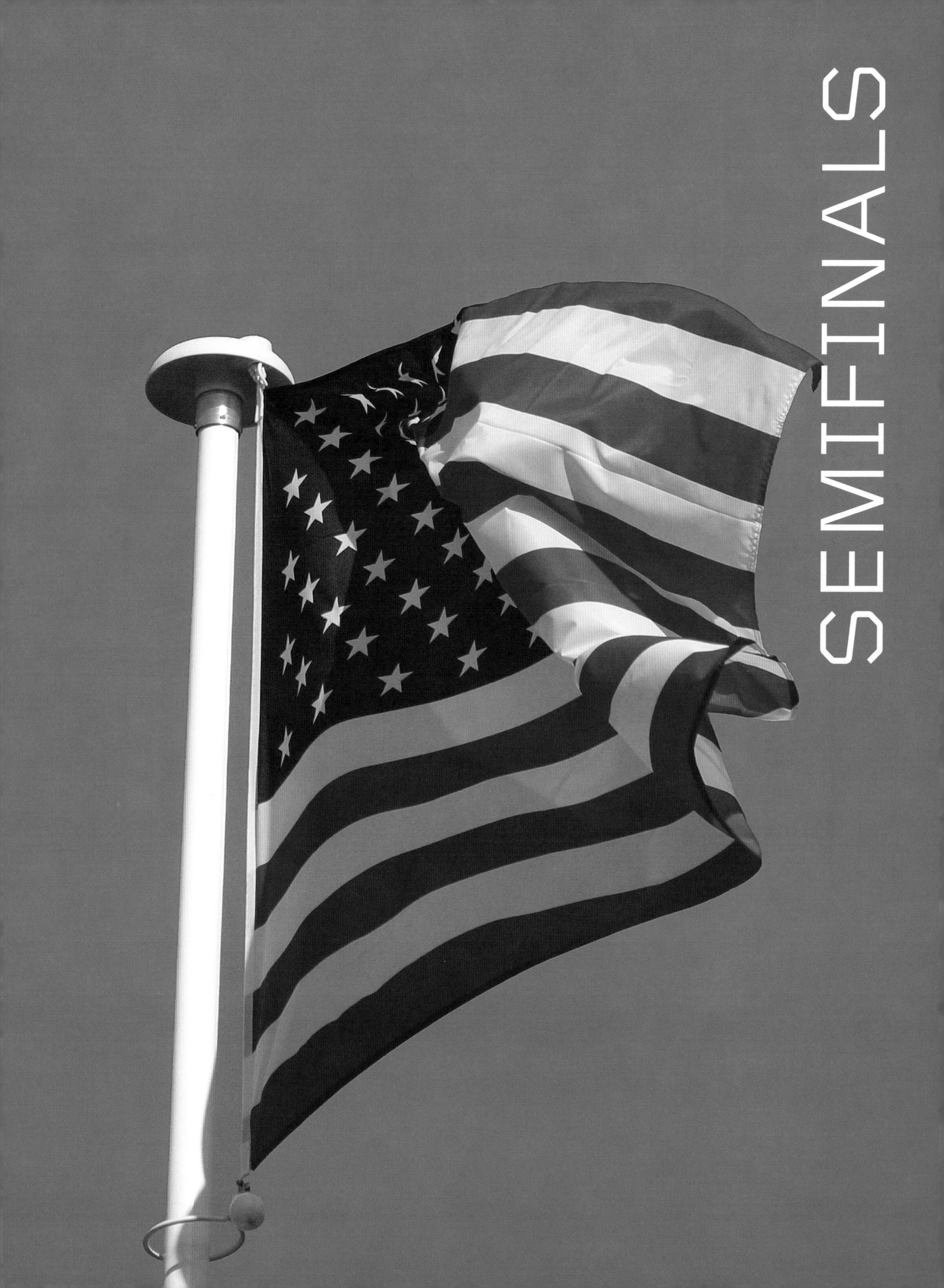

FRANCE V USA

Summer was releasing its grip, foreshadowing autumn. The ochre tint of Roland Garros glowed ever more resplendently than in springtime when all Parisian life descends upon the broad expanse of the Avenue de la Porte D'Auteuil. The Davis Cup was returning to the ancestral home of French tennis, built for *Les Mousquetaires*, who danced and darted their way to sporting immortality.

There was something magical about the decision of the French Federation to take the semifinal against the United States to this special place. The new Davis Cup sponsors, BNP Paribas, loved it, of course. The ambiance was bound to lift the French players and unsettle the visitors from America.

"I think it's wonderful to play such a big nation of tennis and in this place," said the French captain, Guy Forget, in a reflective mood on the eve of the tie. "This stadium was built for Davis Cup, for Mr. Cochet, Mr. Borotra, Mr. Lacoste, and Mr. Brugnon to play against Bill Tilden and his friends from the United States. Now we are back, almost eighty years later. The house will be full and if the sun is still up, I don't think there could be anything better for French tennis and for the Davis Cup."

The imprints Forget had made on the competition since taking over as captain were everywhere, not least in the fact that the Cup itself was housed at the French HQ, also located at Roland Garros. Every home player in his right mind wanted terribly to be a part of Forget's nominations.

Patrick McEnroe, too, had steadied the U.S.A. ship after the brief, boisterous reign of his elder brother, John. As a precursor to the tie, the United States Tennis Association revealed that they had signed him up for another two years at the helm.

"Under Patrick's leadership, we have had a great run the last two years and have won three consecutive ties," said Merv Heller, USTA president and chairman of the board. "There has been a great foundation created for the future of the U.S.A. team, primarily due to his efforts."

At thirty-six, he was the thirty-eighth American captain in the 102-year history of the event. He pronounced himself delighted to maintain such a legacy. "I'm looking forward to the rest of this year and hopefully two more matches, and the next two years. Obviously the goal is to win the Cup. We've got a pretty good shot to do it this year and onward for the next couple of years.

"In moving forward and looking ahead toward the match, our four-man team will be Andy Roddick, James Blake, Todd Martin, and Mardy Fish. We've got the youth movement, and the old warhorse in Todd, who has always been there and is looking forward to taking to the doubles court and, who knows, singles if necessary. We're certainly excited about going over to Paris and accepting this challenge."

There to greet them was Forget and his team of Arnaud Clement, Sebastien Grosjean, Fabrice Santoro, and Michael Llodra. Clement and Grosjean (the best of friends since they first met up as juniors) had faced each other once more in a Grand Slam at the US Open a couple of weeks earlier. Clement had emerged victorious in a five-set replica of their 2001 Australian Open semifinal.

OPPOSITE: Guy Forget congratulates Sebastien Grosjean (**RIGHT**) on sealing France's place in the Final. Arnaud Clement (**BOTTOM LEFT**) gave the home team a winning start, but there were mixed fortunes for American James Blake (**TOP LEFT**).

Neither Clement nor Grosjean had set the world on fire in 2002, having reserved their best tennis for the Cup. Grosjean, to be fair, had been suffering from a long-term back problem that exacerbated any jolts and strains in other parts of his anatomy.

Roddick and Blake meanwhile had not delivered as well as they had wanted in New York. Roddick fell under the spell that Pete Sampras cast over the proceedings, while Blake came to grief, but not before he had given the world number 1 Lleyton Hewitt a decent run for his money.

Roddick did not mind where he played, nor did he worry about the conditions underfoot. "I feel good. I'm getting used to the clay all over again," he said after the second day of practice in glorious conditions. "I feel like I am hitting the ball well, striking it well. It's just a matter of getting used to the points and the way they develop on clay. These are the best clay courts in the world here. It's a pleasure to play on them.

"The French picked the surface that they felt that they had the best chance on. That automatically favors them. The great thing about our team is that every person in the locker room wants to be here. This is priority for everyone on our team."

Blake, too, had no fear that the events would be too much for him to handle. He had played Grosjean at Roland Garros and had defeated Clement the previous summer. "That actually was a big turning point in my career. Before then, I had never beaten a top 20 or top 30 player. I have good memories against Clement but tough memories against Grosjean.

"Roland Garros is a wonderful place. My parents brought me here when I was twelve years old and it is one of the thrills of tennis to be out here as a player. The place has so much history. And being around here, especially with Jim Courier, well, it's an education for me to see how much respect the players have for this place. If I have to play three matches in three days, I'm ready. I always have confidence in myself."

He would need it all. The opening day would pit Roddick against Clement; Blake against Grosjean. Although Roddick had played a dead rubber against Switzerland in Basel in his Davis Cup debut, Blake had never played a Davis Cup match on foreign soil before, and what a place to have chosen for such a baptism.

The emphasis was on the French not to mess up, for they had superiority in terms of experience and local knowledge. Clement took a while to come to grips with this notion and, by the time he had taken in where he was and what was expected, he was 4–0 down in the first set. Little did the crowd know then that he would not be broken again for the rest of the match.

Initially, the Court Philippe Chatrier, named after the greatest modernizer in the sport, was not full of French voices. The one thousand fans with the stars and stripes painted on their faces were giving full vent to their support. It was like a home away from home, and Roddick's early form simply lent greater weight to their vocal backing.

Roddick served for the set at 5–2 but a couple of stinging backhand passes from Clement interrupted the twenty year old's flow, albeit temporarily. At 5–4, he did not make the same mistake again. The French knew, if they had not already suspected, that they were in a match.

Clement knew he had to do something to rattle his opponent—so how about starting to mix the game up, be more aggressive, throw in the odd killer drop shot? He tried all of this, and still Roddick held three break points at 4–4. However, the American got a touch ahead of himself, and went for too much. In the resulting tiebreak, Roddick held two set points, but was denied by a service winner on the first, and a brilliant forehand on the second. The Frenchman then came up with an exquisite drop volley at 6–7 and squeezed France back into the tie.

Roddick, covered in clay after a fall, redoubled his efforts. Indeed, he held a set point at 5–4 in the third only to drive a forehand long. At 6–5 he had four more points to take the set but Clement unfurled some irresistible shots—including a second serve ace—to deny him. Taking the set merely gave him the platform to up his tempo in the fourth and give the French first blood.

For Blake, having to play the French number 1 took on an even greater resonance. He looked anxious, he played anxiously, and by the time many patrons had returned to their seats after a break from the first match, Grosjean led 6–4, 6–1 in the second singles.

At 3–3 in the third set, Roddick came back to urge on his compatriot. "We are down but we are not out," he had said to the media. "The next three matches are all winnable." Blake might have proved the validity of that comment but, having won the third set in a tiebreak, let a 4–1 lead slip in the fourth. Grosjean held steady in the face of some captivating play, and once he had hauled himself back

Todd Martin and James Blake **(SECOND RIGHT)** kept the United States in the hunt, but Andy Roddick's **(SECOND LEFT)** two defeats by Arnaud Clement **(RIGHT)** and Sebastien Grosjean **(LEFT)** proved decisive.

in at 5–5, the confidence drained from Blake's face. "It's the most disappointed I've been in my life," he said. "I'm just going to have to try to find a way to forget it."

The next afternoon Blake was called in to replace Fish in the doubles and partner Martin. Once more, doubles was raised to a spellbinding level we so rarely see across the world at regular tour events. The first set was pocketed by Santoro and Llodra in twenty-eight minutes. Martin, Llodra, and Blake were all broken at the start of the second, and when Santoro broke the sequence, a 3–1 lead should have been the foundation upon which to build a tie-winning advantage. But Santoro, strangely, lost his serve to bring the scores level at 4–4. The Americans took the set on a tiebreak, but France responded, winning the third set 6–2.

Here was the moment for Blake and Martin to dig deep and rally around the flag. Whether or not they felt Santoro might be the weaker link, it seemed they had more opportunity on his serve and he was duly broken. Blake held firm when serving for the set, drawing errors from both of the Frenchmen.

It was the same story in the fifth. As the decibels mounted in concert with the pressure, Santoro stumbled in the ninth game. Though Martin was 0–30 down as he served for the match, the young and old in the American colors played each point on its merits, did not panic, and brought their one thousand followers to fever pitch with the victory that brought them back into the tie.

"After the singles, when I was so distraught, this is such a thrill," said Blake. "If it comes down to me in the fifth match, I will work hard, do my best. It's nice to feel that winning feeling again."

Unfortunately for Blake, it was too little, too late. He was not to get his chance. Grosjean, desperate to lead his country back to the Final after losing both singles in Melbourne the previous November, beat Roddick in four sets 6–4, 3–6, 6–3, 6–4. Yannick Noah was there to revel in the atmosphere, which was much like it had been at Roland Garros in 1983 when he won the French title. Grosjean said: "When I needed the public they were there for me." The cockerel was still crowing.

ABOVE: The French supporters were in fine voice at Roland Garros.

OPPOSITE: French hero Sebastien Grosjean is lifted aloft by his teammates.

JOY FOR RUSSIA
AS ARGENTINA IS EDGED OUT

RUSSIA V ARGENTINA

Where does one begin to tell this story of Marat and Machiavelli, of Yevgeny and yo-yo tennis, of Argentina and absolute anguish? Only when the curtain had come down on three days in Moscow that will never be forgotten by those who participated, watched it live, or even followed the scores on the Davis Cup website, could we begin to piece together an extraordinary semifinal.

Russia qualified for its first final since 1995, when Marat Safin defeated the Wimbledon finalist David Nalbandian 7–6, 6–7, 6–0, 6–3 and collapsed into the arms of his captain to scenes of tumult rarely, if ever, witnessed around a tennis court in this city. Safin had never known emotion like it, not in front of his own people. He was accorded a place in Russian affections he had could not have believed he would ever reach.

It seemed likely to end this way, though what the story would have been if Argentina's number 1 player Guillermo Canas had been fit to play, is one of those intriguing nuances that this competition throws up every year. It is hard to believe the tie could possibly have been any closer than it turned out.

As if it didn't have everything else, the tie included a six-hour-and-twenty-minute doubles match between Safin and Yevgeny Kafelnikov against Nalbandian and Lucas Arnold. The contest was only two minutes short of the all-time record Davis Cup match, between Mats Wilander of Sweden and John McEnroe of the United States in St. Louis in 1982, in which the American prevailed 9–7, 6–2, 15–17, 3–6, 8–6 in six hours and twenty-two minutes. Only the introduction of the tiebreak prevented the doubles from topping that figure, though it became a Davis Cup record of its type.

It is not surprising that, from Friday morning until deep into Sunday evening, people were walking around in a complete daze. And there were those—the brave Gaston Gaudio to the fore—who could not walk at all. For the Argentines, this was the learning curve, touching points they had never touched before. Most had never played a Davis Cup tie outside their own country, and a carpet court in Moscow was hardly designed to make them feel at home. It didn't exactly feel great under Safin's feet either.

The choice of ground and surface might have been determined and cloaked as a mutual agreement, but in Moscow, that meant Yevgeny decided. Safin was not exactly enamored, but he knew better than to complain. No point in that.

Safin opened against Juan Ignacio Chela, fresh from a fourth-round appearance at the US Open and tagged as one of those players on the verge of a real breakthrough. The match was as tight as one would have expected, Safin having to recover from losing the first set tiebreak 7–1 to eke out sets two and three. He cruised in the fourth, but it was simply a tasty hors d'oeuvre to the courses to come.

"It was a tough match," Safin said. "I was nervous at the beginning because I was playing in front of my home crowd. It's not my best surface and I'm suffering because it is really fast, the bounce is very low and that means I put more pressure on myself to play each point really well. I had so many break points I couldn't make. It's difficult to keep your focus when that happens. There was a lot of pressure, a lot of pressure. You just have to do everything you know to win."

OPPOSITE: Wimbledon finalist David Nalbandian (**BOTTOM LEFT**) made a winning debut for Argentina, but Yevgeny Kafelnikov (**TOP LEFT**) and Marat Safin (**RIGHT**) took Russia through to the final.

Lucas Arnold and David Nalbandian's **(LEFT)** record-breaking doubles victory was not enough to save Argentina, following earlier defeats for Juan Ignacio Chela **(SECOND RIGHT)** and Gaston Gaudio **(SECOND LEFT)**. Former president Boris Yeltsin **(RIGHT)** joined the Russian team in celebration.

If the crowd had gotten itself into a state over Safin's victory, it was nothing to the levels of frenzy that would greet the next two matches. Kafelnikov against Gaudio proved to be one of those remarkable singles matches, one that twisted this way and that, following nothing like a discernible pattern, and being won and lost between sheer magic and utter exhaustion.

Kafelnikov must have felt he had it in the bag at two sets to one. Then he played a loose game at the start of the fourth and gave Gaudio the impetus to set off on a surge. "I was so mad at myself," said Kafelnikov, "because I was feeling so good after the third set and I let it go." Before he had time to get himself mentally readjusted, Gaudio had taken the fourth set 6–2 and was racing toward two match points at 5–2, 40–15 on his serve in the fifth. "I looked at Kafelnikov's face and it was for sure he was broken," said Alfredo Bernardi of the Argentine daily, *La Nacion*.

Gaudio went for an ace down the middle and was certain he had made it, but French umpire Pascal Maria decided it was a fault. What a moment to choose for such a decisive call. On his second point, a forehand drive was judged to have gone a centimeter or two long and, at that, Gaudio's left leg locked. He was cramping from tip to toe.

Of the final thirty-one points of the match, the Argentine won five. He could not move, and Kafelnikov seized the chance and bolted for the finish line. "I didn't know that I had the energy to do it," he said later. "I don't recall such a match as that in all that I have played in the Davis Cup. It was … a big epic."

But no bigger than the one that would follow the next afternoon. Russia was 2–0 in the lead and it was felt that they had to go again with Kafelnikov and Safin, while Alejandro Gattiker, the Argentine captain, had a fresh combination up his sleeve, Nalbandian and Arnold, making their debut as a doubles team in Davis Cup.

It might all have turned out very differently had Arnold not missed a backhand return on break point at 4–4 in the third set. The Argentines had taken the first two sets 6–4, 6–4 and a point then may well have settled matters. Instead, the four players would remain on court for another four hours. And, once more when his country needed him, Kafelnikov endorsed his reputation as the iron man of the modern game. Once Arnold's backhand missed, the impetus shifted and it was his serve that buckled, a netted volley giving Kafelnikov the chance to win the set with a crunching forehand service return. Nalbandian then double-faulted to lose his serve, giving Russia a 2–0 lead in the fourth and they duly served it out to 6–3. What followed was one of the momentous sets in the competition's history, all three hours and five minutes of it.

Incredibly, break points were at a premium, Safin saving one at 2–3 and Nalbandian one at both 8–8 and 10–10. When the Argentine saved two more at 12–12, the Russians began to have doubts as to whether this would be their day. As these things go, it was Nalbandian who double-faulted to lose his serve at 16–16, allowing Safin—who had won his previous four service games to love—to serve for the match. At 40–30, Arnold saved the first match point with a winning backhand return; on an advantage point, Nalbandian came up with an extraordinarily deft angled backhand volley. The ball was back in the Argentine court.

Serving at 17–18, 15–40, Kafelnikov saw his partner save the first match point against them with a brave smash, only to put a forehand volley into the net on the second for Argentina to cherish an improbable 6–4, 6–4, 5–7, 3–6, 19–17 victory.

Arnold could not praise his partner enough. "David is a great singles player who has not had much experience of doubles, and today he played the match of his life," he said. "He never doubted us for a moment, even when Safin was serving out of his mind in the fifth set." Up in the press seats, Alfredo Bernardi and his colleagues were awash with emotion and had some idea how the players felt. "After six hours and twenty minutes in the same seat, we all had cramps as well. We could not move. It was the most incredible match I had seen in twelve years covering tennis," he said. "What emotions there were in the stadium and for long into the night."

What would the teams be on Sunday? Kafelnikov said he had the desire to play but not the physical energy. "But this is what sport is about. I will tell myself that today we missed a good chance but I need to try to be ready."

The walking wounded convened in their hotel lobbies on the final day for a head count. Gaudio insisted he wanted to play, but the team doctor, Javier Maquirriain, would have nothing of it. "It is impossible for you to go out there," the doctor said. And so Gaudio bowed to the inevitable, leaving Gattiker to choose Nalbandian for the first reverse singles against Safin. At precisely the same moment, Shamil Tarpischev, the Russian captain, was making the announcement that Kafelnikov could not play a decisive rubber. Exhaustion had overtaken Mr. Inexhaustible.

"In 2000 we weren't playing well and were defeated by Spain. In 2001 I had a back injury when we lost to Sweden. This year EVERYTHING FITS, so we must convert our chance."

MARAT SAFIN (RUS)

The first two sets of Safin versus Nalbandian, as if in keeping with the extremes of the tie, went to gut-wrenching tiebreaks, the first Russia's way, the second to Argentina, though Safin had squandered a 4–2 lead midway through the set. And then, from somewhere deep in his soul, the twenty-two-year-old Safin found a new burst of energy that was too much for his twenty-year-old opponent. It was as if someone reached into him, found two dead batteries and replaced them with live ones.

Safin won the third set 6–0, only for Nalbandian to grit his teeth and fight back in the fourth. When Safin seemed likely to get to grips again, a couple of linesmen began to have their say. Nalbandian was foot-faulted—the first anyone could remember—and was thrown off his stride. Safin pounced. To a deafening crescendo of noise in the Luzhniki Palace, he served out for the match and a place in the Final. "Finally we made it," Safin said. "This is really nice.

"I thought we were unlucky in the doubles. We should have finished the match in three days and ended up playing one match more than six hours. I wasn't feeling well before this match, I have to tell you. But we had no other choice. It was me or nothing. We could not really play (Mikhail) Youzhny, he does not have the experience.

"I told myself 'Marat, you have to win.' In the end, I think I was playing my best tennis and yet, in the doubles, I was suffering from cramps. I'm not really that good physically right now but I suppose I am twenty-two and there is enough in my body to see me through. I found the power to finish the match and to win for my country."

The Argentines could have no regrets. The players had never been this far in Davis Cup before. They were representing a country in a state of economic chaos and low morale, and were forced to play on a court not of their choosing, without their strongest player. And they came close, very close. Had it gone to a fifth rubber, the tie would probably have been theirs.

Their captain Alejandro Gattiker was sad in defeat, but promised better days to come. "We have so many good young players in Argentina—their time will come." But not, sadly, with him in the captain's chair. The depressing economy at home meant that Gattiker could not afford to turn down the opportunity to coach Mariano Zabaleta full time. And Zabaleta, remember, could not even get into this side. With his career replenished, Canas fit, and Guillermo Coria pushing from the sidelines, what price Argentina in 2003? The fact that they chose as their new captain, a man with an inappropriate surname, Gustavo Luza, should not be counted against them.

ABOVE: There were mixed fortunes for David Nalbandian, whose marathon doubles victory was followed by a four-set loss to Marat Safin.

OPPOSITE: Safin at the moment of triumph.

PROFILE: MARAT SAFIN

BORN | JANUARY 27, 1980, IN MOSCOW, RUSSIA

TURNED PROFESSIONAL | 1997

DAVIS CUP RECORDS | SINGLES 11–10 | DOUBLES 6–3

Marat Safin has been known to give an interview that the journalist would have to struggle to hear. He would sit with his peaked cap pulled down low over his eyes, his hand across his mouth, and mumble a few words that didn't really add up to very much. And yet this is a man who can be the most engaging company, who can keep press conferences enthralled with witty, usually self-deprecating remarks, and an abundance of good humor.

It is this sheer unpredictability that makes Safin so enjoyable, so mercurial. Who can know in what state of mind they are going to find him, what he is going to say, how he is going to react to the most innocent of questions. When he won the US Open in 2000, having shown complete imperturbability when ripping through a formidable field, he treated the assembled media throng to the finest Russian vodka and a cartload of iced prawns. He went on to finish that year as the number two player in the world. Number one awaited him, surely.

He has all the strokes, as well as a beautifully fluent game, based on flawless technique and unsound temperament. It is an absorbing combination, one that excites and exasperates in equal measure. For a big man, he seems to have so much time; a clean, undisturbed rhythm; and an absurdly easy balance. It has come to him naturally from an unnatural beginning.

His mother, Rausa, had been his coach from the ages of six to thirteen, but the opportunities for a tennis player in Russia were few and far between. The decision to leave behind his country and embark on a solo journey to Rafael Mensua's tennis camp in Valencia, Spain (backed by a Swiss bank that took a terrifically risky investment), opened Safin's eyes to the wider world, and to his fluency in the Spanish tongue.

"I chose to leave Russia and try to be a tennis player and when I did it, it was really, really difficult to leave the family and move to a country where you don't know anybody, you don't know how to speak the language," he said. "But sometimes you have to make decisions that you don't want to make, but I needed it when I was fourteen. Tennis in Russia has changed so much since those days. Now we have everything: balls, racquets, and people for practice, but before it was so difficult because of the situation in the country."

The image of Russian tennis, which received a boost from the equally enigmatic Yevgeny Kafelnikov, has been further enhanced by Anna Kournikova on the women's side and Safin on the men's. There are just as many women intrigued by Safin as there are men who would like Kournikova's picture on their bedroom wall. He is exactly the kind of disorganized rebel who leaves more questions than he answers. Safin thrives on his image as a suave guy who gives only just enough away to leave the people wanting more.

GREAT BRITAIN d. THAILAND 3–2 | Birmingham, Great Britain • indoor carpet
GERMANY d. VENEZUELA 5–0 | Karlsruhe, Germany • indoor hard
ROMANIA d. SLOVAK REPUBLIC 4–1 | Presov, Slovak Republic • indoor carpet
BELGIUM d. ZIMBABWE 4–1 | Harare, Zimbabwe • indoor hard
SWITZERLAND d. MOROCCO 3–2 | Casablanca, Morocco • outdoor clay
NETHERLANDS d. FINLAND 4–1 | Turku, Finland • indoor hard
AUSTRALIA d. INDIA 5–0 | Adelaide, Australia • outdoor hard
BRAZIL d. CANADA 4–0 | Rio de Janeiro, Brazil • outdoor clay

QUALIFYING ROUND

GREAT BRITAIN V THAILAND

It had to come down to Team Tim and the Paradorn Party, as those heavily involved in the build-up to this romantic Davis Cup by BNP Paribas World Group Qualifying Round had long suspected. Would the shoulder of Henman, the British number 1, be able to stand the strain of the three matches in three days he would almost certainly have to play to give his side a real chance?

Could Srichaphan possibly maintain the form that had carried him—as if on some magic carpet—through the American summer season to his highest world ranking of number 31 and inspired him to his first ATP Tour title, the Long Island Classic, the Sunday immediately preceding the US Open?

The preparation of the British team, in a state of flux already, was further disrupted when news came through on the Monday before that Greg Rusedski was pulling out with a miserably timed foot injury. There was, therefore, an even greater need for Henman to be ready for the task at hand.

Henman did not flinch from the prospect, indicating that if the shoulder he had strained badly in Indianapolis should be in reasonable shape, he would drag himself out there for the country's cause. Some felt it was a terrible risk. The captain, Roger Taylor, said, partly tongue-in-cheek, "It's not Tim I'm worried about, it's the rest of the team."

The Thais, seeking a place in the World Group for the first time in their history, did not want to make too much of their hosts' misfortunes, but Srichaphan said that maybe the news gave them a chance of making the tie close. Even he did not envisage quite how close it would become.

The initial creakiness in Henman's play against Danai Udomchoke was not unexpected, given that he had not played a match in eighteen days, spending most of that time worried about what would happen when he did play. His first delivery of the match, a 100 mph serve, came searing back past him and gave the twenty-one-year-old Udomchoke the promise of victory in a set he could not have imagined he would win. But he would need more than a set to defeat the determined Henman.

"Most of this is mental," Henman said after his 4–6, 6–3 6–3, 6–2 victory over Udomchoke, a wiry little customer who packed a penetrative backhand. "Physically, I feel really good but the next eighteen hours are pretty important. The reaction (from the shoulder) is there was no reaction. I do feel cautious—it's tough to place absolute trust in it. I've been pushing it harder and harder and when I serve, as in the first set today, I was waiting for something to happen."

Martin Lee's jaw was firmly set as he attempted to avoid a thrashing from Paradorn Srichaphan, but he could not invade the air of serenity that has enveloped the Thai number 1 ever since he stepped on Andre Agassi's toes in the second round of this year's Wimbledon. Srichaphan wasted no time bringing the scores level, though Martin Lee, Rusedski's fill-in, contributed to his own downfall, double-faulting five times in a fifteen-minute first set, eventually falling 6–0, 7–6, 6–2.

Britain chose two twenty-eight year olds for the doubles, Henman and Miles Maclagan, the latter having spent a year off the circuit, coaching Zimbabwe's Wayne Black, before getting itchy feet. Henman and Maclagan had played together a couple of times, although they couldn't remember where or when. When they lost the first set to Srichaphan and Udomchoke, some doubted the wisdom of the captain's choice but, once again, Henman proved them wrong. He was a tower of strength. Maclagan got carried along on the tide and they wore the Thais down in four sets.

Once again, the pundits wondered if Henman would be fit to play. And he was fit to burst, playing as well as he had done all year to thrash Srichaphan 6–3, 6–2, 6–3. "It was massively satisfying," he said. "I pretty much produced the goods and that's what it's all about in Davis Cup. There was no way I thought I was going to play three matches.

"The way it has turned out, I think it is probably, no definitely, one of the best."

OPPOSITE: Tim Henman **(RIGHT)** overpowered Paradorn Srichaphan **(TOP LEFT)** to seal Britain's victory against Thailand, having earlier won a vital doubles rubber with Miles Maclagan **(BOTTOM LEFT)**.

ABOVE: Daniel Udomchoke failed to capitalize on a one-set lead against Henman.

GERMANY V VENEZUELA

This was supposed to be one of those uneventful, straightforward matches that underlined the momentum Germany was gleefully gaining under the new captaincy of former Wimbledon champion Michael Stich. Then came an exhibition in Berlin and the wheels on the applecart of German Davis Cup hopes fell off.

Stich played his former nemesis Boris Becker in front of a capacity crowd riveted by their old rivalry revisited. After the match, Stich wondered what Becker thought of the prospect of playing doubles in the Davis Cup, an event in which both of them had excelled but Becker's contribution was legend. Becker suggested the captain had better run that humdinger past those members of the team already guaranteed their places. "And, surprise, surprise," Becker said, "they didn't think much of the idea."

No, indeed, Rainer Schuettler, Nicolas Kiefer, and Tommy Haas were almost apoplectic. Their response was so vigorously anti-Becker that Stich, who had really wanted Boris back in the fold, was moved to resign his post as captain after less than a year in control. And so there was going to be another upheaval in the German Davis Cup camp and a new captain in Patrik Kuehnen.

After this contretemps, a home tie against Venezuela in Karlsruhe was going to prove to be very small beer, and the Germans aren't exactly enthusiastic about small beers. Indeed, there can rarely have been a more one-sided match in the history of World Group Qualifiers than Germany's 5–0 thrashing of a side containing a group of players who would probably walk unrecognized down the streets of Caracas.

The Venezuelans managed to muster twenty games from five matches, and six of those came in the first reverse singles, when Kepler Orellana had the effrontery to stretch Kiefer to 7–5 in the second set.

It seemed as if most of the personalities involved had something other than this tie at the back of their minds. Patrik Kuehnen, brought in to steady the ship, wondered whether he would win the blessing of the German Tennis Federation for an extended period in charge. For Haas, it was the health of his parents who had both been seriously injured in a traffic accident in Florida earlier in the year. Both were making significant progress but it was nevertheless a terribly disconcerting time for the player who was keen to establish himself among the very best in the world.

This would not be one of those occasions when Haas had to dig deep into his repertoire to succeed. Schuettler had put the Germans into an early ascendancy with a supremely confident victory over Jose de Armas, and Haas wasted little time disposing of Jimy Szymanski in straight sets. "I knew Jimy from our junior days and though it looked a pretty easy match on paper, I could not afford to give anything less than 100 percent of my concentration and commitment," he said. "I was pretty happy with the way it all came together."

Indeed, the Germans came together brilliantly all weekend. Kiefer and David Prinosil won the doubles emphatically to bring the curtain down on one of the few ties at such an important stage of the event to finish in three straight-set matches without a single break of serve. A forty-five-year-old Becker would probably have won the tie playing with one arm tied behind his back, but the Davis Cup career of the thirty-four-year-old former world number 1 was now officially over. There was no way he could earn a place back. Haas, Schuettler, and Kiefer, if they stayed together in body and spirit, promised a fine team indeed. Kuehnen was happy to have his name put forward to lead them.

"A relegation tie is always dangerous, no matter who you are playing," he said. "I had to convince the players to go out on court with the right concentration and preparation, and what we saw was all four guys playing their finest possible tennis. They were all very professional. For the moment, my own intentions are a secret—we shall see how it turns out."

OPPOSITE: New German captain Patrik Kuehnen looked on as Rainer Schuettler, Tommy Haas (**RIGHT**), David Prinosil, and Nicolas Kiefer completed a 5–0 whitewash over Venezuela.

ABOVE: Jose de Armas collected only three games against Schuettler in the opening singles.

GERMANY ENSURES SURVIVAL
AS VENEZUELA IS OVERWHELMED

SLOVAK REPUBLIC OUSTED AS ROMANIA RETURNS TO TOP FLIGHT

SLOVAK REPUBLIC V ROMANIA

The last time the world's media had taken note of Andrei Pavel was during this year's Roland Garros, where his quarterfinal against Alex Corretja was interrupted by rain. He returned to the locker room to learn that his wife was in the first throes of labor, and drove from Paris to Germany to witness the birth of his son. He then drove back to the French capital where the security man on the gate wondered who this disheveled figure was arriving at six in the morning.

Not surprisingly, Pavel, who fell asleep on a sofa in the lounge and had to be shaken awake to come out onto court a few hours later, was beaten by Corretja, but nevertheless walked off to a hero's ovation. The Grand Slam semifinal that is certainly within him would have to wait.

By the time he stepped out in the less rarefied atmosphere of Presov in the Slovak Republic, Pavel had spent some time at home with his young son, and, refreshed, was eager to try to secure Romania its place among the top Davis Cup nations. It was a tall order.

In Dominik Hrbaty and Karol Kucera, the Slovaks had two wily campaigners, and Karol Beck had proved both in Davis Cup and on the ATP Tour that he was a young talent to be taken very seriously. Pavel was well aware that he and his team would have to be at their best.

"We have a very good team right now," he said. "We get along, there is a good chemistry there, the best I have known it in Davis Cup. We knew we were in for a difficult match, especially as Kucera, who had said that he wasn't going to play just a week before the tie, had changed his mind."

The decision clearly inspired Hrbaty, who accounted for Adrian Voinea in the opening singles in four sets. This result did not trouble Pavel unduly, given the emphatic nature of his start and finish against Kucera, a match he won 6–0, 6–3, 6–7, 6–2 to level the tie at the end of the opening day.

Then followed another doubles match of sustained brilliance over the better part of an afternoon. Pavel teamed with Gabriel Trifu against Hrbaty and Beck. "To tell you the truth, I have never played a match like this before in my life," Pavel was moved to admit afterward.

He is happy to gloss over the first four sets—two of them tiebreaks—and get straight into the teeth of the fifth. He was serving for the match at 5–4 and lost it. At 5–6, Trifu was down 0–30 in his serve "but he held his nerve and served big at the right time," Pavel said. "I got lucky with one volley that touched the top of the net." Then it was Beck's turn to serve, only for the Romanian pair to produce a couple of clean winners that undermined the confidence that had been swelling on the opposite side of the net.

The second time it fell to Pavel to serve for the match—" I said to myself, this time you have to go for it"—he did not falter and, after four hours and five minutes of consummate tennis, Romania led 2–1. Pavel was, thus, another of the top quality players of the world asked to play on three successive days in order to cement the prospect of victory.

He did not flinch from the task. His opponent Hrbaty broke early in the opening set of the first reverse singles and had points for a double break. However, when it came time for the wiry Slovak to serve for the set, he missed a couple of elementary groundstrokes, tossed in a double-fault, and Pavel forced a tiebreak.

The Romanian played the perfect breaker, hitting three aces and a couple of clean return winners to clinch it 7–1. Once Hrbaty had been broken early in the second set from a 40–0 lead, the tie was all but in Romania's pocket. Pavel was, once more, the toast of his country.

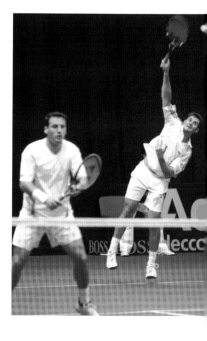

OPPOSITE: Dominik Hrbaty (**BOTTOM LEFT**) defeated Adrian Voinea (**TOP LEFT**) to give the Slovak Republic an early lead over Romania, but his loss to Andrei Pavel (**RIGHT**) consigned the home team to defeat.

ABOVE: Pavel and Gabriel Trifu won a five-set thriller against Karel Beck and Hrbaty.

ZIMBABWE V BELGIUM

Though these continue to be hard times for the host country, Zimbabwe's tennis brotherhood and its astonishingly resilient Federation president Paul Chingoka staged a Davis Cup tie that left an indelible impression on those fortunate enough to have been there.

Zimbabwe put on a brave face to the outside world (or in this case, Belgium) in a Qualifier that paraded every bit of fun and ferociously committed support that has come to be the norm in Harare. There may have been doubts about what the country stood for in so many political ways, but as a sporting host, it deserved nothing but praise.

Xavier Malisse was not the first (and would not be the last) foreign sports star to feel a little bit weak in the pit of his stomach as he flew into the capital. Tennis players are experienced travelers, and the team from Belgium knew what was going on, or at least as much as they were allowed to know from a national media that reputedly lived in constant fear of retribution if it uttered a word out of place. "But we didn't see one piece of violence, nothing bad at all," Malisse said. "We didn't go out at night into the city of course but we wouldn't do that in many places. I admit I was a little scared, we all were. I watch a lot of CNN, I follow what is going on."

But once more, there was an oasis of calm at the Sports Centre a couple of miles out from the middle of the capital. The practice sessions were not just there for the players but for Zimbabweans to get into the rhythm of the dancing and chanting that are a constant, unnerving backdrop for the visiting sides.

Malisse had never experienced anything quite like it. "There is always noise in Davis Cup, and you sense it more away from home, but these were perhaps the toughest conditions I have ever played in, because it seemed to be all the time. They just didn't rest," Malisse said. "And they keep drumming until the moment you are about to toss the ball to serve, which can easily take away your concentration."

To have Malisse's name drawn out of the hat first to face the younger of the Black brothers, Wayne, was a significant boost for Belgian prospects. Except that Wayne Black came out in a mood of total defiance, recovering from the loss of the first set on a tiebreak to win the second in similar fashion and then, twice, stand a point from the third.

"It was then that I started to serve really well and mentally I became really tough," Malisse said. "Having won a lot of important matches this season from difficult positions, I think that definitely helped me. It is hard to play at your best with all the stuff happening around you, the noise and the interruptions. So I was really pleased the way I fought back."

Not only did Malisse win in four, but he was out at the side of the court to witness a performance from Olivier Rochus that was every bit as impressive as his defeat of Marat Safin in the second round of Wimbledon last year. Though Byron Black, in the final throes of his international career, took the first set in another tiebreak, he was swallowed up by a sea of winners off the ground from the younger Rochus, whose brother Christophe was not selected for this tie.

The Belgians sensed they were unlikely to win the doubles. The Zimbabwean combination of Wayne Black and Kevin Ullyett boasted a Grand Slam notch on their title belt, and they duly defeated Gilles Elseneer and Tom Vanhoudt, although the Belgians did manage to win a set.

Malisse came back the following day to defeat Byron Black in straight sets. He said at one stage that he was mentally exhausted and wondered if he could carry on. But this being Davis Cup, he endured and became Belgium's hero. "I was spent physically, I was mad with some line calls but I held it together," said Malisse. "I love the competition."

OPPOSITE: In his final Davis Cup tie for Zimbabwe, Byron Black **(BOTTOM LEFT)** lost both singles rubbers against Olivier Rochus **(TOP LEFT)** and Xavier Malisse **(RIGHT)**.

ABOVE: Kevin Ullyett partnered Wayne Black to a four-set doubles victory against the Belgians.

BELGIUM RETURNS
TO WORLD GROUP
AFTER ZIMBABWE TEST

FEDERER SHINES AS SWITZERLAND TRIUMPHS OVER MOROCCO

MOROCCO V SWITZERLAND

How often the mind plays tricks. Roger Federer could not get one face out of his mind, one he wished would come toward him smiling, every time he turned a corner in Casablanca. Through a sea of friendly African faces, with traditional fezes atop their dark skin, through the harsh rays of the Mediterranean sun and through the din that accompanied his every move, Federer could see Peter Carter.

It was not surprising once you knew the whole story. Carter had been instrumental in guiding the teenage Federer's tennis career. An Australian who had lived in Switzerland for a long time, Carter had fostered a relationship with the young man that would last a lifetime. But Carter's life was tragically cut short by a road accident in South Africa earlier this year.

Federer had not been playing well in the American hard court season and could have used a rest. He would have done anything to avoid flying back home for the funeral but, of course, he needed to be there. It was an awful experience.

"I owe him so much," Federer said. "Peter taught me about the sport and growing up and it is a terrible waste to have lost him so young."

Federer seemed to be coping pretty well when he returned to the circuit in New York, losing in the fourth round of the US Open to Max Mirnyi of Belarus. The next test would be as arduous as they come.

Morocco away on clay in the Davis Cup was sure to strain all of Switzerland's resolve and yet, as it turned out, the victory they achieved was stunning in its both its quality and brevity.

There was not a hint of one-sidedness in the opening match when Younes El Aynaoui sprang back from the indignity of losing the first break of serve in the tie to sweep aside Michel Kratochvil 7–5, 6–2, 6–2.

From the start of his match against Hicham Arazi, it seemed as though Federer was in a different world, a tennis trance, in which he was able to strike the ball, however it came to him, as clean as a whistle. He was calm in a competition whose very essence is the state of madness that surrounds the majority of its matches. Arazi is a dangerous player who can overwhelm his opponents, seemingly just for fun. But not this time. He was obliterated in three sets and won only six games in the process. Federer was simply awesome. Whether it had to do with the promotion of his current coach, Peter Lundgren, a Swede, to the post of temporary director of the Swiss team, or that his old coach was somewhere in his mind, controlling affairs, the player could not be sure.

"I felt I had to be in a very good mental state today, and I was very happy with my performance," Federer said. "I was solid from start to finish. I knew I was going to play three matches and once we lost the first one it was important to get us back to 1–1. I love doubles as much as singles, so tomorrow holds no fears for me."

Nor did it need to. In partnership with George Bastl, Federer swept through another straight-sets performance, this time against El Aynaoui and Karim Alami to the disbelief of a crowd who expected their fellow countrymen to establish more of a bridgehead on home soil. But never had they seen someone as possessed as Federer.

On Sunday morning, against the top-ranked Moroccan El Aynaoui, Federer tore into his work, winning 6–3, 6–2, 6–1. It was as sublime a performance as he had given in Davis Cup, and there had been a good few, as he had virtually single-handedly defeated the Americans in the opening round of the 2001 competition, spoiling captain Patrick McEnroe's debut. Lundgren simply said: "Roger is a very special player." There was no doubting it.

OPPOSITE: Roger Federer **(RIGHT)** overwhelmed Younes El Ayanoui **(TOP LEFT)** to complete Switzerland's win over Morocco to the delight of captain Marc Rosset **(BOTTOM LEFT)**.

ABOVE: Hicham Arazi was also outplayed by Federer on the opening day.

FINLAND V NETHERLANDS

OPPOSITE: Raemon Sluiter's (RIGHT) victory over Jarkko Nieminen (TOP LEFT) paved the way for the Netherlands, with Paul Haarhuis and Sjeng Schalken (BOTTOM LEFT) clinching the decisive point against Finland.

ABOVE: The Dutch team celebrates with its fans.

Of the many players grappling for the points, momentum, and recognition needed to enter the world's top twenty, few had made a more emphatic impact in 2002 than Finland's Jarkko Nieminen. The left-hander from Masku, who had started the year ranked number 61, had bounded up almost thirty places and done much to invigorate Finnish tennis. Now came the telling moment. How could he cope with having to lead his nation into the World Group at home, but against the country that had reached the semifinals the previous year?

"This is going to be a very different experience for me but I have a strong feeling for the Davis Cup. I know Finland wants a good experience and I hope I can provide it," he said. It was a tough task.

Sjeng Schalken was among the most improved players in the world, a semifinalist at the US Open, a quarterfinalist at Wimbledon, and someone who could be inspired to glorious heights when the mood took him. His singles partner Raemon Sluiter was a player who couldn't seem to hack it on the tour but came to life during Davis Cup. Who could forgot those images of him weeping as he was led from the court in Rotterdam as Holland's dream of a place in the 2001 Final fell away?

There were to be no tears in Turku, the venue chosen by the Finns. Not Dutch ones, anyway. Sluiter opened the tie against Nieminen, a match the home side suspected it had to win to stand a fair chance of progress. It was a roller-coaster ride of a match: tiebreaks, love sets, brilliant surges, and deep dips. Nieminen struck first, clinching the opener in thirty-two minutes and taking Sluiter to a second-set tiebreak, only to crumble under a welter of wonderful returns from the Dutchman, whose double-fisted disguise, sweet angles, and drop shots contrived to confuse the Finn.

That set lasted an hour. The third was over in twenty-five minutes, with Nieminen obliterated. He recovered to break Sluiter first in the fourth set but the Dutchman rallied again, forcing a tiebreak that contained eighteen points, some wonderful tennis, and, ultimately, proved the strength of Sluiter's desire.

"This was such an important match for us and I played some of my very best tennis today," Sluiter said—comments to which Nieminen could only concur. "When the big shots had to be played, Raemon played them," he said. "I had no complaints but this leaves us with a very difficult situation."

Schalken has made a habit of getting himself involved in long, drawn-out matches. The 20–18 final set at Wimbledon 2000 against Mark Philippoussis exhausted everyone involved, and he had driven Lleyton Hewitt to the point of despair on the grass this year before falling in five sets. It was not totally unexpected, then, that he should be taken to a 15–13 tiebreak by Tuomas Ketola in the second rubber. Once he had disentangled himself from that inconvenience, Schalken dominated in the manner he might have expected, his 7–6, 6–3, 6–3 victory more or less ensuring that the Netherlands would secure their place in the top echelon again.

Once the evergreen Paul Haarhuis, in partnership with Schalken, had taken care of Ketola and Nieminen in straight sets in the doubles, the Dutch were in a buoyant mood. Captain Tjerk Bogtstra could not hide his delight at his side's victory. "We didn't really know what we could expect from Finland, because Nieminen has improved so much and playing at home means it is so different, but I always know I can trust my players absolutely. Sluiter and Schalken proved again what excellent players they are in Davis Cup."

DUTCH TOO STRONG
AS FINNS MISS OUT

AUSTRALIA V INDIA

Each morning after rising, Leander Paes sinks into a deep meditation and visualizes the day's matches: his opponent, strategies, points, the court color, the way the wind will blow, and the crowds that may be cheering against him.

Paes tried to envisage India rising from their far lower world rankings to upset Australia at Memorial Drive, Adelaide, and win back a place in the World Group in what might be his final year on the tour. However the twenty-nine-year-old doubles specialist and his young teammates were unable to blank out a far greater vision.

Lleyton Hewitt, the world number one, had come home for the first time in nine months to set matters straight and ensure that Australia would not be shut out of the World Group in 2003. "I'm not thinking of this as 2002," Hewitt said after he had steamrollered Harsh Mankad in straight sets on the first day of singles play. "We've got five matches to win the Cup again and this is a start for us." And, as India found to their cost, Hewitt simply lives and breathes the special aroma of the championship.

With Hewitt, Australia has more than half a chance. It is about building a team capable of sustaining a challenge in the World Group. India, on the contrary, is at a crossroads with a long-term plan to build its side from emerging players like Mankad, Rohan Bopanna, and Sunil Kumar Sipaeya, the teenager tasting the special delights of the competition for the first time.

"You need that experience and the only way you're going to get it is to be in those situations," the Indian captain Ramesh Krishnan said. "Leander is slowly petering out—I think this is toward the end of his career. Mahesh [Bhupathi] also. They have been occupying center stage for so long that some of our youngsters have not been able to get into that position. When that happens there is going to be a lull."

Australia knows only too well what those lulls feel like. For now the outlook is promising. Australian captain John Fitzgerald is encouraged by what he sees in the distance, namely the fast-improving talent of Wimbledon junior champion Todd Reid and US Open junior semifinalist Ryan Henry, both seventeen.

"In the junior teams at the moment, we're looking reasonably good," Fitzgerald said. "You don't want to get carried away. There's a long way to go. They don't just fall off trees. There's a good program in place and they've been working at this for several years now and they're starting to get a few results, but they're quiet achievers and that's what I like."

Australia duly sealed victory with a day to spare. Thirty-one-year-old Wayne Arthurs buried some Davis Cup demons with a workmanlike 6–4, 3–6, 6–3, 6–4 victory over Paes, before Hewitt and Todd Woodbridge clinched the decisive point in the doubles. Both small men, they broke serve as predicted and held their own serves throughout the 6–3 7–6(5) 6–1 victory over Paes and Vishal Uppal.

Arthurs, who had lost the deciding rubber in last year's Final, admitted, "I just wanted to get a little bit of a monkey off my back from Melbourne and here I had a very good opportunity to do that."

Australia's eventual 5–0 clean sweep served two purposes: first, the proud Davis Cup nation was saved from relegation to the Asia/Oceania Group 1 competition. Second, Hewitt and Woodbridge had paired for the first time in doubles and liked the chemistry. "I'd love the opportunity to play with Lleyton in a few tournaments if we could work it out, because that could only make us better," Woodbridge said.

The Australians will need a solid doubles pairing if they are to make a claim on the Cup next year. The talk in Adelaide was that new parent Patrick Rafter was highly unlikely to make a return, something the public was still hoping for until the 2002 Australian of the Year made an official statement to the contrary.

OPPOSITE: Lleyton Hewitt **(RIGHT)** led Australia to victory over India, while compatriot Wayne Arthurs **(BOTTOM LEFT)** banished his Davis Cup demons with a four-set triumph over Leander Paes **(TOP LEFT)**.

ABOVE: India's Harsh Mankad went down in straight sets to Hewitt.

BRAZIL V CANADA

The prospect of Canada winning a place in the World Group was a touch fanciful, even before they knew they would have to face Brazil and on a court designed not to help the Canadians one iota.

For starters, Canada does not have a singles player anywhere near the caliber of the opposition. Daniel Nestor, the mainstay of the team for a long time, traveled the world making a living from excelling at doubles. That prowess might come in very handy if Canada could win even one singles victory on opening day, but it was an order taller than the Sugar Loaf mountain.

In their ranks, the Brazilians had the former number one player in the world and national institution, Gustavo Kuerten, and a former Roland Garros semifinalist, Fernando Meligeni. As backup was Andre Sa, who had given Tim Henman such a difficult time in the quarterfinals at Wimbledon.

From the outset, it was clear that the Canadians were going to have their work cut out for them. In the first rubber Meligeni held steady after a third-set lapse against Frank Dancevic, leaving Kuerten and Nestor to take center stage.

Nestor, whose singles ranking has dropped more than six hundred spots in the past few years because of injuries to his shoulder and elbow, opened strongly to break Kuerten in the second game. A chastened "Guga" regrouped in the fourth game, breaking back and gaining in confidence to take the first set 6–4.

In the second set, the hard-hitting pair exchanged breaks and nailed ace after ace to set up a tiebreak, where Nestor took an early 3–1 lead. With the Canadian's elbow starting to flare up, he was unable to convert four set points and hit a return into the net on the twenty-second point of the tiebreak, falling two sets adrift.

In the third set, Guga took advantage of Nestor's lack of power, taking cheap points from a weakened serve, and breaking the Canadian three times to secure a 6–4, 7–6, 6–0 victory. Afterward Nestor said: "I had a lot of adrenaline in the tiebreak, and when I lost it, I felt really deflated, but that was no excuse for my performance in the third, even if I was hurting. I'm sure Guga wasn't at the top of his game, and I wasn't at mine either."

Kuerten concurred. "The second set was a crucial one. I saved four set points, which is maybe why the match changed so much from the second to third set. He lost his confidence and I took advantage of that. If he had won one of those set points, the outcome could have been very different."

In the doubles, Nestor played for the first time with twenty-four-year-old Simon Larose. It's not easy to adjust to a new partner in such a critical match but Larose did not let the side down.

Larose, resplendent in red bandana, helped Nestor hold up Kuerten and Sa—also a first time pairing—for three hours and twelve minutes before the Brazilians emerged victorious at 4–6 7–6(5) 6–1 4–6 6–2 to guarantee their survival in the elite 16.

"It was the first time we played together in Davis Cup," said Kuerten, "so we didn't really know what to expect and how to react after points. But we really found our rhythm in the middle of the second set. We really began to believe in each other and that was the moment we felt we would beat them, however well they played."

It did not help the Canadian cause that the match was played on a slow clay court in periods of drizzle that slowed the balls down and made generating any pace a difficult chore. The delight of the Rio fans was palpable at the end, with another tilt at the crown itself.

OPPOSITE: Brazil was too strong for Canada on home soil, with Fernando Meligeni **(TOP LEFT)**, Gustavo Kuerten **(RIGHT)**, and the Kuerten/Andre Sa pairing **(BOTTOM LEFT)** wrapping up victory with a day to spare.

ABOVE: Frank Dancevic suffered a four-set defeat by Meligeni in the opening rubber.

BUOYANT BRAZIL RETAINS WORLD GROUP STATUS

PROFILE: TIM HENMAN

BORN | SEPTEMBER 6, 1974, IN OXFORD, ENGLAND

TURNED PROFESSIONAL | 1993

DAVIS CUP RECORDS | SINGLES 22–6 | DOUBLES 8–5

A SMALL VILLAGE IN OXFORDSHIRE called Weston-on-the-Green has every reason to be proud of its heritage. It can lay claim to being the birthplace of England's best tennis player in six decades.

Tim Henman is very much the embodiment of Middle England. He is well-spoken and polite—attributes that poor judges might mistakenly regard as inherent weaknesses in the cut-throat world of professional tennis. However, Henman has strongly countered the pressures of the unrelenting desire for British success, spending years as one of the world's top ten and reaching four Wimbledon semifinals.

From the minute they could walk, Henman and his two elder brothers were rivals at everything. When eight-year-old Tim was taken to a tennis club in Middlesex run by former international David Lloyd, the sparks began to fly.

Lloyd, who was determined to beat the British Lawn Tennis Association at their own game, enlisted Henman as one of the second intake in a private scheme sponsored by the financier Jim Slater, in which a group of prodigious kids boarded at Reed's School in Surrey. "My parents were somewhat cautious about me going away to school, but I was really adamant," Tim said. "I was totally involved there from eleven to seventeen. I suppose you can say I didn't come up through the authentic route, but because no one has come through any other way, there's not much to compare it with.

From there, he was nurtured by the LTA men's national manager, Bill Knight, who decided Henman should be one of four players sent across the world with David Felgate as coach. Within a short space of time, Felgate noted something special in Henman—nothing he could determine there and then, but he knew the kid with the shock of black hair was different.

From the moment Felgate and Henman split away and decided to work together, the player's ranking shot up. His classical serve-and-volley game stood him in special stead at Wimbledon—a tournament he had first visited at the age of eight—as a trend-breaker against the predominance of groundstroke proponents in the sport.

He has a special affinity for Davis Cup, too. Heading into 2003, Henman has never been on the winning side in a World Group tie, something upon which he has set his heart. He has been the mainstay of the British team for the past six years, capping it off with a heroic performance in Birmingham against Thailand when, dogged by a bad shoulder, he played three matches in successive days to steer his country to victory. "He is a captain's dream," said Roger Taylor.

Henman became a father for the first time in October when his wife Lucy delivered a daughter, Rose Elizabeth, at eight pounds, four ounces. That it will change his life is certain; that it might change his attitude to tennis, we will have to wait and see.

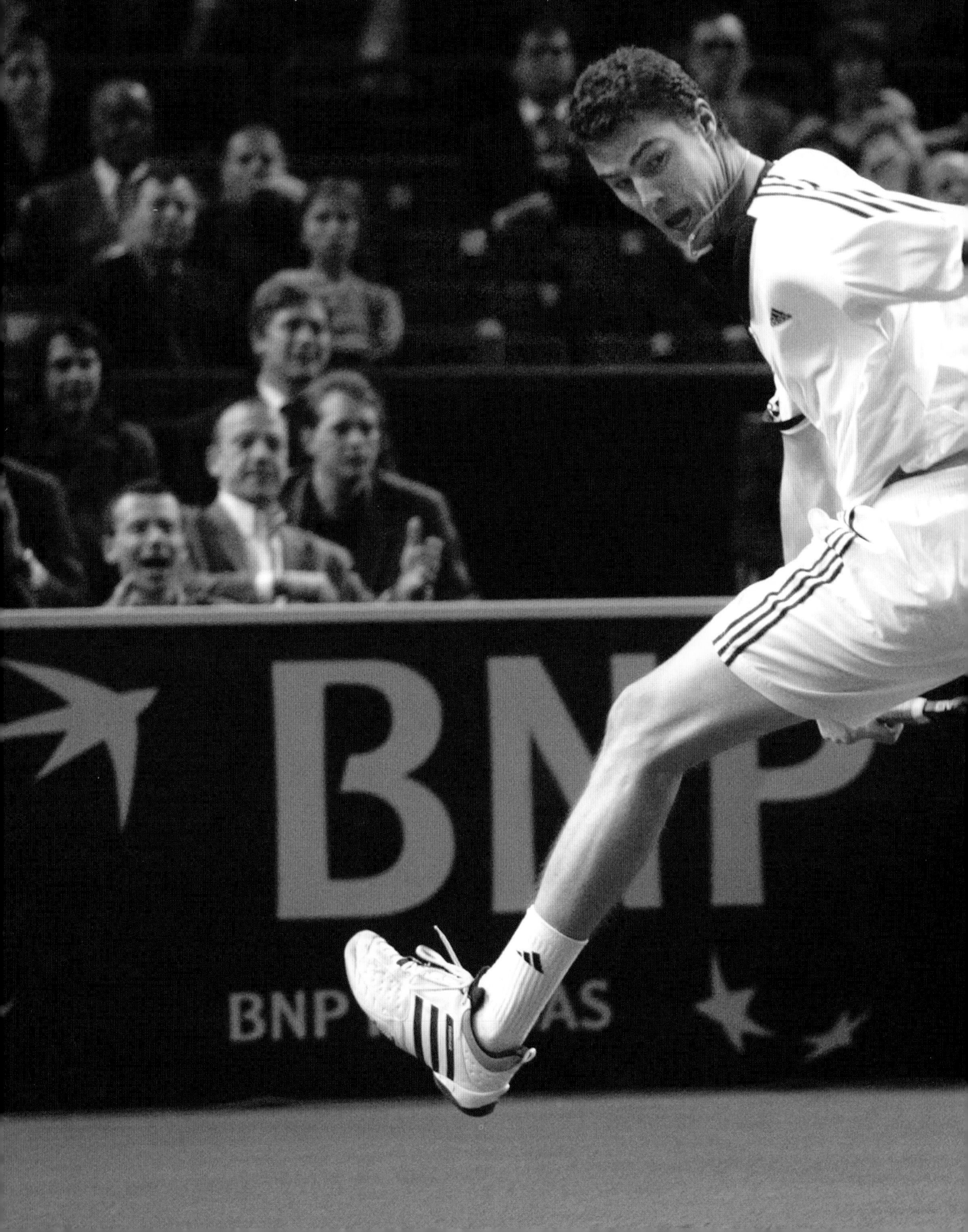
BNP
BNP

FINAL ROUND

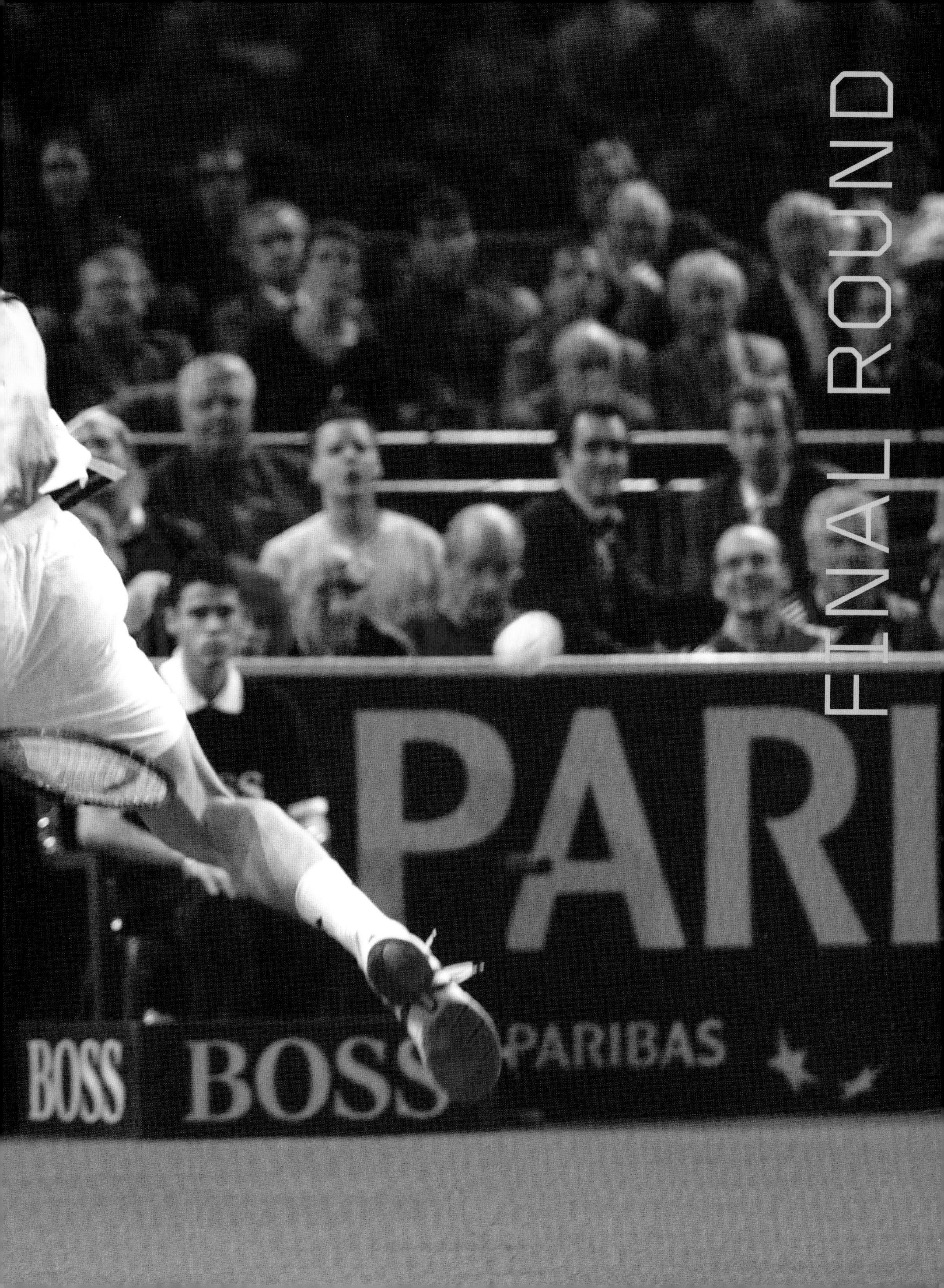

FINAL ROUND

Mikhail Youzhny opened his tennis year in the warmth of Qatar, losing in straight sets to compatriot Nikolai Davydenko. It is doubtful that the two young men's conversation that evening turned to Davis Cup, but it is certain that the next time they meet they shall talk of little else. In the depths of the Russian winter eleven months later—Moscow was sixteen degrees below zero the Sunday night of the final—what better to warm the cockles of the heart than the extraordinary events of the ninetieth Davis Cup Final. This became one of the most historic, a magnetic meeting of the most successful nation of contemporary times—France—against one that had never before carried off the famous silver bowl. Ultimately, it became Youzhny's story. It is a story of how a career—even an existence—can be transformed in twenty-four hours. How a player can walk gloriously unnoticed along life's pathway one day and the next day, through the sheer force of his spirit and determination, see his name carved forever in the annals of his sport.

Youzhny woke up on the morning of Sunday, December 1, thinking he would be sitting in the second row of the Russian bench, urging his compatriots, Marat Safin and Yevgeny Kafelnikov, to redeem a situation that looked all but lost for Russia. France, the hosts, were leading 2–1 after Saturday's doubles. Then came a call from the captain, Shamil Tarpischev for Youzhny to be ready to play in the fifth match.

A victory might not have been possible if Sebastien Grosjean, the French number one, could have accounted for Safin in the first reverse singles. The Cup would have been back in the tender care of the nation that had taken the splendid trophy to its heart so fervently in recent years. Seemingly the French wished the Cup to take up permanent residence at the home of the president of France, the Elysees Palace. The Cup even had a new and deeply committed French title sponsor in BNP Paribas, the bank for a changing world.

But Safin had different ideas. There was hardly a place on the map that the twenty-two-year-old had not visited in the last five months of the year. He was determined to guarantee his place in the Tennis Masters Cup, but not at the expense of helping Russia secure another, more recognizable Cup for the first time in its forty years of participation.

Safin stopped off in Moscow for the semifinal against Argentina, winning his two singles and joining Kafelnikov for a memorable doubles against David Nalbandian and Lucas Arnold that wrote another chapter in the history of the event. He would probably have to do the same in the final for Russia to win. Safin's fellow Davis Cup stalwart Kafelnikov had gone on record again in the build-up to the event, saying he would step down if Russia won the final. The twenty-eight-year-old from Sochi had talked about possible retirement all year, and not just at Davis Cup matches either. One of the many times he mused about it was after he had been humbled by Dominik Hrbaty in the US Open, two weeks before the semifinal.

OPPOSITE: Sebastien Grosjean and Marat Safin enjoy a break from practice.

ABOVE: Safin and Yevgeny Kafelnikov were expected to carry Russian hopes in the Final.

Yevgeny Kafelnikov **(LEFT)** was making his third final appearance, but Arnaud Clement **(RIGHT)** was left out of the French team for the second successive year. Marat Safin **(SECOND LEFT)** went on to give Russia an early advantage with a four-set victory over Paul-Henri Mathieu **(SECOND RIGHT)**

"Perhaps I did [put all my eggs in one basket for Davis Cup], but I don't want to see that as an answer to my results. I already said I have one goal for myself for the rest of the year and that is to win Davis Cup, but not without giving such effort for any other tournament. But it seems like it is happening this way. But believe me, it's not what I feel inside. I feel like I'm trying very much every single match I go in. But it's just not there. Confidence is not there. And perhaps it all started in Australia this year where I also lost in the second round, in a similar type of a match to what I had today. And that kind of set up the whole season like that. But [if we win the] Davis Cup, will I retire? Definitely."

Having spent years listening to Kafelnikov, one was still not sure how seriously to take him, although the word "definitely" had a ring of certainty to it. He had announced in the build-up to the final that immediately after it he would head to a Zurich clinic for an operation on a varicose vein in his left leg. There was no doubt as he practiced with Safin on the afternoon before the draw ceremony, that Kafelnikov was not in the best of spirits. When the teams and their coteries arrived at the opulent Hotel de Ville for the draw ceremony, he looked extremely distracted.

The buzz, though, was about the complexion of the French team. There appeared on the stage a curly-haired, brown-eyed youth one could remember having seen somewhere before. Was it not Paul-Henri Mathieu, the young guy who had given Andre Agassi the fright of his life in the fourth round of the French Open at Roland Garros before succumbing in five pulsating sets? Here was a turn-up for the books.

The French captain, Guy Forget, had pulled a rabbit from the hat. Mathieu played idly with a sponsor's bauble depicting a snowswept Eiffel Tower, not the least bit fazed by the flurries of amazement greeting his elevation from the lowliness of number 147 in the world less than twelve months earlier to a pivotal role in the final.

Mathieu, exhausted from his endeavors playing for Lille in the French Inter Club Championship at the end of 2001, admitted he had slept through the last final, when France triumphed on a portable grass court in Australia. That victory had provoked an open-top bus ride for the champions down the Champs Elysees and champagne buffets with the president. If the twenty-year-old from Strasbourg could inspire his nation to their fourth victory in twelve years he would surely merit a cavalcade all his own.

There had been rumors circulating the stadium on Wednesday that Mathieu might replace Arnaud Clement in the final reckoning, but when Forget announced his four-man side, it was to whistles of skepticism. Of the five players who had made their Davis Cup singles debuts in the final round since it was introduced in 1972, only John McEnroe won his match and that came against Great Britain's John Lloyd in Palm Springs in 1978.

Mathieu might have played in the semifinal against the United States at Roland Garros, when Forget was torn between his potential and a back injury that was wearing down his number one player Sebastien Grosjean. When Grosjean said he would be all right—and his two singles victory justified such optimism—Forget relented, though he described Mathieu as "a pearl." Mathieu had gone on to win back-to-back ATP titles in Moscow (where he defeated Safin in the semifinals) and Lyon, a triumph consolidated by a success against the former world number one, Gustavo Kuerten. The moment Clement said he didn't feel that his right wrist, troubled with tendinitis, would stand the prospect of two five-set matches across the weekend, the skipper had no hesitation in calling upon Mathieu.

"The captain told me before dinner last night that I was in the side," he revealed, though he did not go on to divulge whether he could actually digest his food upon Forget's choice. "I think I am perfectly prepared for such a match.

"The image I have of the Davis Cup was the 1991 final (he was nine) that I watched on television. I didn't see last year because I was sleeping through the night but I was with them in my heart. Tomorrow is going to be different, because this is no longer a dream, this is reality."

Safin suggested Mathieu took risks during their match in Moscow because he had nothing to lose and that, this time, with all of France breathing down his neck, it would be very different. The French beginner bridled. "I don't know why he said that, because it was my first semifinal, so there was pressure there too," he said. "Why should anything be different tomorrow? It's going to be a tennis match and I'm going to try my best."

If he didn't believe that Davis Cup was really any different, perhaps Mathieu had the proper attitude to overcome the pressure. But Davis Cup has long been recognized as a competition that shattered nerves and systematically unraveled people's games and, while Mathieu wanted to treat his debut as just another crossing of the white line onto the court, it proved to be much easier to say than to carry through.

There are times, in Davis Cup, when choices made in good faith cause splits in relationships that take an awfully long time to heal. Fabrice Santoro, carried shoulder-high by the then captain Yannick Noah on the occasion of his fifth-rubber victory against Australia in 1991, was subsequently dropped from the next match and could barely bring himself to speak to Noah for the next ten years.

One of Forget's lieutenants, Thierry Tulasne, in an admission that highlights the selfless spirit now pervading French tennis, said he had ended up supporting the United States in the 1982 final in Grenoble. "When our captain, Jean-Paul Loth, came to my room to tell me I was being dropped from the singles in favor of Henri Leconte, I went into shock," Tulasne recalled. "I found it terribly unjust. I had played all the previous ties. Sitting with my teammates when the matches started, I found myself wanting the Americans to win. I was very young but I had a very developed ego. I regret my reaction and I can only admire the way the team behaves today.

"Arnaud (Clement) has had to suffer the disappointment of being dropped for both the final in Melbourne last year and now this time. But after Guy has told the player concerned, all of us, the coaches, the doctors, gather around and offer support. It happened to Nicolas Escude in the semifinals and to Michael Llodra here. They all have the right attitude. No one is bigger than the team."

It is the prevailing attitude that every successful Davis Cup country has, and France had become one of the very best in the recent history of the event. This was their fifteenth appearance in the final (called the Challenge Round until 1972), and, more significantly, their fifth in twelve years since their memorable victory over the United States in Lyon in 1991.

As it had been the previous year in Melbourne, when the Australians believed their best bet was to install a grass court over the Rebound Ace of Rod Laver Arena, so the French felt that improvisation on a grand scale was their route to victory. The concept had, of course, blown up in the Aussie's faces in 2001, but Forget believed the FFT's decision to bring in truckloads of Roland Garros–like red clay and spread it across the Palais Omnisports de Bercy was the right one for France.

"For each tie there are difficult decisions to make," said Forget. "It just so happens that this time the surface was not easy to choose, the reason being that the guys on our team have very different styles and different surfaces on which they are known to play well. The decision had to be made and the player majority had its day. And it is true that the Russians are probably less dangerous on clay than they would be on a hard court.

"I don't think I need to protect this team, the guys are independent, each player knows what has to be done and everyone's role is well defined. The pressure from the media is good, it is needed for the high profile of the event, it pushes the guys to surpass themselves and produces really good tennis. They will optimize their games and their qualities but they will be totally serene. They all have lots of experience."

Serene was hardly the word as the players were introduced on the opening day. For a start, the president of the Republic, Jacques Chirac, was in attendance, along with the former president of

RUSSIANS CREATE HISTORY
AS FRANCE FAILS
IN TITLE DEFENSE

Russia, Boris Yeltsin, and his wife, who were to watch every single nuance of the three days.
A gentleman in a tuxedo belted out the Russian anthem; the French team linked arms around their
shoulders to the spine-tingling rhythms of La Marseillaise.

Mathieu was first up against Safin, about as tough an assignment as one could anticipate on one's
debut. Indeed, he started without an apparent nerve in his body, causing Safin to slip over on the soil
in the first game, holding serve and leaping back to the bench in the manner of someone who would
not be fazed, whatever fate would throw his way. Indeed, it required Safin to come up with three
brutish serves, none of which Mathieu could return in court, to ward off three break points in the fourth
game. It was going pretty well for France until the seventh game inevitably conjured a turning point.

With a ferocious forehand service return, Safin secured his first break point, though Mathieu saved
it with a whipped backhand crosscourt that caused the Russian, for the second time, to lose his footing
and crash into the clay. Dusted down and directing his gaze once more at a second serve, Safin belted
an unstoppable backhand return winner and then drew an unforced forehand error from Mathieu to
secure the final's first break. An ace on his second set point and the visitors were ahead.

But Mathieu had not been battered—far from it. Forget got back inside his head and was delighted
to see his man embark boldly into set two. Despite missing a relatively simple backhand overhead in
the second game that could have really rocked him, Mathieu steadied his nerves and came dashing in
behind a deep approach to put away a backhand volley on his first break point. The rubber balloons in
the all-blue section of the crowd behind the French bench were being beaten together with a renewed
gusto. Indeed, Safin had to see off three break points for Mathieu to take a 4–0 lead and three more
when serving to stay in the set at 2–5. When he netted a backhand on the first set point in the ninth
game and the match was tied, a scent of real drama filled the air inside the cavernous Palais.

Yet, whatever the situation in a match, Safin's gait does not change. His shoulders roll, he ambles
across the baseline, and he gives nothing away. Before Mathieu had time to enjoy being back in the
match, Safin rifled his way to a 5–0 lead in the third set—a couple of double-faults at crucial times not
helping the French cause—and snaffled it 6–1. There was then a perceptible increase in the intensity
level. Mathieu, as is his wont, grunted on every shot, but where there had been silence as Safin
executed his shots as clean, clear explosions, he was suddenly breathing a touch harder, extracting

ABOVE: Nicolas Escude and Fabrice
Santoro **(RIGHT)** made a stunning
Davis Cup debut to defeat Yevgeny
Kafelnikov and Marat Safin **(LEFT)**
in a five-set thriller.

OPPOSITE: Santoro at the moment
of triumph.

"I'm so happy, I'm so glad. I cannot describe what I'm feeling right now. It's just something that is just so great, it's the best."

MARAT SAFIN (RUS)

every last ounce of effort. It was not too much of a surprise that he should break to lead 2–1 with a couple of crunching forehand winners. Although he missed a relatively straightforward forehand that would have extended his lead in the fifth game, he was at Mathieu's throat again to take the seventh with another forehand that picked up a puff of dust from just within the baseline.

Serving for the match at 5–2, Safin eased to 30–0 but played a couple of loose shots and was back at 30–30. He double faulted on match point. A forehand crosscourt winner from Mathieu gave him a break point, one he joyously claimed by stepping into a backhand service return to nail it down the line. The noise was deafening. Safin tripped and fell for the third time in the match as Mathieu dug deeper still, holding for 4–5. Serving for the match for the second time, Safin scuffed an easy forehand put-away at 15–15, and the French were on their feet, exhorting their man to find a way. But Safin had that little extra, firing a service winner to take him to match point number two, and nailing the point with an ace. He had won 6–4, 3–6, 6–1, 6–4, inspiring Mathieu to say: "I think today he was the best player in the world. When he plays like that, it's really tough. If I had played at my best who knows what would have happened, maybe we would have put holes in the balls."

The torch was, thus, passed to Kafelnikov, given just the start he would have wanted. And how hard was it for Grosjean, knowing he had lost his two singles in the final a year earlier, to have to start his quest in the knowledge that if he lost, the final was as good as in the opposition's pocket? A big question mark hung over Kafelnikov's attitude. Christopher Clarey wrote in the International Herald Tribune: "(Kafelnikov's) repeated insistence that he will retire are strange words from a world traveller and frequent gambler who has yet to win Wimbledon or the US Open. Strange words, too, from a man who has already entered the 2003 tournament in Doha, Qatar. But Kafelnikov has long marched to his own drummer, covering his tracks and mixing his messages and overloading his schedule year after year with singles and doubles matches despite repeated warnings from his coaches and advisors.

"That quantity over quality approach has helped his bottom line, he has earned approximately $22 million, a career total surpassed only by Pete Sampras, Andre Agassi, and Boris Becker, who all won more major titles than the Russian. But despite his recent efforts, he still looks a kilogram or four over his ideal playing weight and though he did win the first of his two Grand Slam singles at the French Open in 1996, he has struggled on clay in recent seasons, a big reason why the French chose indoor

clay for the final when their own players are more comfortable on hard courts." Grosjean, a French Open semifinalist in 2001, had wasted six match points the last time he appeared in this particular stadium, in the BNP Paribas Masters, a month earlier against Carlos Moya of Spain. He may have forgotten those blemishes as he stepped out to face the veteran Kafelnikov in the second rubber, but when he lost his serve to love in the fifth game, the French number one needed a good talking to from his captain. Forget did not miss his trick.

Grosjean bounced back immediately and then raced to three set points at 0–40 in the tenth game. The veteran's response was emphatic, extracting a couple of errors from Grosjean against far better depth and then placing a smash away to secure the bridgehead at deuce. Holding there, Kafelnikov did so again to take us into the first tiebreak of the final.

There, Kafelnikov wilted, double-faulting to go down 4–2, netting a forehand on the next point. Though he put away a smash to retrieve one of the mini-breaks, he was left without a defense to a thumping off-forehand, which Grosjean plays better than most players in the world.

Any thought that the second set would be a repeat of the first, when Grosjean broke to love to lead 3–2 and instantly forfeited the advantage, disappeared in humiliating harness with the complete breakdown of the Russian's game. From 3–3, Kafelnikov did not win another game as Grosjean embarked on a nine-game frenzy and completed his 7–6, 6–3, 6–0 victory with a thirty-two-minute final set that was one of the more brutal half-hours on court that Kafelnikov has ever had to endure.

Once more, then, the final would continue into Sunday but, looking at an emotional Kafelnikov on the Friday evening, it didn't seem certain he could last into a third day. "I could have gone another three sets," he said, "but unfortunately, it did not last that long. I'm not tired, I'm ready. The question is if I can put a hundred per cent performance like I always do. It's a different thing.

"I was quite happy that Marat won the first match, to give me the kind of freedom that I was playing without such pressure. But, on the other hand, I was maybe not thinking about how to approach every point. I wasn't really paying too much attention to the score. I was just trying to play my best game. Sometimes, when you do that, you make mistakes. That's what I did. It is understandable."

What had to be understood now was perfecting the art of doubles. The team of Santoro and Escude had never played together before in Davis Cup; Safin and Kafelnikov had partnered each other in seven

Marat Safin **(LEFT)** levelled the tie with a straight sets triumph over Sebastien Grosjean. Grosjean then joined his teammates **(SECOND LEFT)** to watch Paul-Henri Mathieu **(RIGHT)** squander a two-set lead against Mikhail Youzhny **(SECOND RIGHT)**.

previous rubbers, and their last together concluded in that monumental 19–17 final set against Argentina in the semifinals. But, however successful, these Russians had never won a Davis Cup tie together in straight sets, and so the odds were that this would be an endurance test for both sides.

From first exchange to last, it was an incredible match. The initial point involved all four players trading volleys at the net where, not for the first time, the French would be the masters. The first three to step up held serve comfortably, Kafelnikov lost his to love and the first set went to France. Santoro felt the pinch at the start of the second, though the rally on break point, which saw him play successive volleys off his toes, deserved better than Kafelnikov's swiping backhand denouement. The French survived a break point for 1–5 but Russia took the set.

When Escude, attempting another audacious smash on the retreat, landed on the small of his back in the third game of the third set, his anguished look raised fears of an injury, not the way anyone would want the festival to end. But even though the French pair once more pocketed the Kafelnikov serve, they could not capitalize and, under increasing Russian bombardment, Santoro lost his in the seventh game and again in the eleventh. Kafelnikov, serving for a two-sets-to-one lead, raced to 40–0, then played a couple of nervous half-volleys to 40–30. But Escude made certain the Russian crossed this particular line, netting a backhand that, nine times out of ten, he would have made.

When he emerged from the locker room for the fourth set, the hero of last year's final was wearing a rubber-ring-like contraption around his midriff as he stepped up to serve. To the groans of his countrymen, he lost it, with a backhand stab from Safin converting the Russians' second break point. But Santoro was now delving deep into his unique repertoire. Lobs on the return of serve; acute, cutting volleys; and remarkable reaches from beneath the height of the net were all used to convincing effect as both Russians lost serve and the French brought the match all square.

How odd that it should be Safin who would wilt in the final set. True he was undone in his first service game by Kafelnikov's poorly timed backhand interception to set up the only break of serve in the decider. Escude went on to serve for the match, showing no trace of nerves as he completed the 6–3, 3–6, 5–7, 6–3, 6–4 victory with a crunching overhead.

Which brought us to young Mr. Youzhny. The twenty-year-old who wrote his name into tennis fable, when history and fantasy mixed in a drama you would insist could never be matched in anything other than the magical, mystical Davis Cup.

ABOVE: Mikhail Youzhny **(RIGHT)** silenced the French crowd **(LEFT)** with an extraordinary comeback against Paul-Henri Mathieu.

OPPOSITE: Mathieu is consoled afterwards by teammate Nicolas Escude.

Here was someone who had never won a live rubber in four ties in the championship, despatched into the deep end of the final on foreign soil, in the fifth and deciding match. Safin had done his bit by sweeping aside Grosjean 6–3, 6–2, 7–6 (the 13–11 tiebreak included the saving of four set points by the Russian to throbbing emotions) and now the floor was being swept clean for someone to mark it with historic footprints.

Looking much older than his twenty-eight years, Kafelnikov had run out of gas. A conversation on the Saturday night between captain and veteran warrior concluded that Youzhny would stand the better chance against Mathieu or anyone else the French might produce. And so he was nudged out to face the massed ranks of the opposition's support against a fellow twenty-year-old who had given Safin a splendid run for his money on Friday. Youzhny had watched Mathieu battle Safin never thinking for a moment that he would be more than a spectator for the final encounter.

Two sets down, Youzhny's backhand—supposedly the gem in his shot-making armory—was all over the place. To get back into the match, he had to snap out of it and so he did. In a manner of such glorious, nerveless, thunderous maturity, Youzhny became the first man in the 102-year history of the championship to win the fifth rubber of the final from two sets to love down. He will dine out on that little accomplishment for the rest of his life.

Poor Paul-Henri Mathieu. At the crushing climax to his 3–6, 2–6, 6–3, 7–5, 6–4 defeat, he could not hold back the tears. They rolled down his cheeks as if a dam had burst. He knew in that instant how Wayne Arthurs had felt a year ago, when he was called upon as a final resort for Australia when Patrick Rafter was ruled out and lost the deciding rubber against Escude on his home soil. Last night, Escude was on the losing side, having triumphed so valiantly in Saturday's doubles. This wonderful event, Davis Cup, is very cruel for the loser.

This is a championship that makes men and can break them. As the silver medal was placed around his neck by the president of the ITF, Francesco Ricci Bitti, Mathieu looked as if he were somewhere else, gazing vacantly at some distant object, trying not to focus on the fixed smile in front of him. He only knew he was playing in the final when the France captain Guy Forget broke the news to him over a dinner on Wednesday night. He probably wished now he had missed the appointment.

Mathieu, called Paulo by his mates, had started so brilliantly, or at least he had profited from the nerves that consumed Youzhny in the early stages. By the time Kafelnikov and Safin had joined the rest of the gang at courtside, Youzhny was a set and 3–0 down, had just served up a double-fault and the captain hardly seemed to know what to say to him. The magic words of encouragement were coming from the row behind, from his brother Andrei and Mikhail's coach of twelve years, Boris Sobkin, who never stopped reminding him—or so it seemed—that he was Russian and the Russians never gave up.

Though Mathieu took the second set, there was still a glint of hope in the eyes of the prickly-haired Youzhny. A glorious backhand that landed smack on the line gave him the edge at 3–1 in the third set

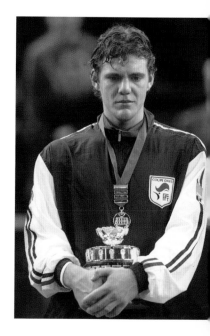

OPPOSITE: Yevgeny Kafelnikov and Marat Safin celebrate Russia's triumph.

ABOVE: Paul-Henri Mathieu fails to hide his disappointment.

and though Mathieu responded with an immediate break back, Youzhny was swinging with a new inhibition and Russia dared to hope that their kid might yet produce the goods.

Mathieu, pumping himself up on the adrenalin from the Russian supporters, drew ahead 4–2 in the fourth set having lost his opening service game. Here, surely, was the platform for him to move on and grant France their fourth victory in twelve years. But Youzhny was to be roused, the backhand was beginning to regularly pierce the French resistance, and a scan at the 2002 results showed he had won the Stuttgart title on clay two weeks after Wimbledon from two sets to one down in the final against Guillermo Canas of Argentina. So Youzhny clearly had what it took but could he call upon it today?

Mathieu was beginning to rock, not roll. He lost the fourth set—though he was two points from victory at 4–5, deuce—and then dropped serve the third game of the decider. Youzhny gave up his own delivery for 3–3, but his response was profound, breaking Mathieu to set up a victory that he secured with a love service game. Captain Tarpischev, who had sat cross-legged and impassive throughout the final game, was first up to embrace Youzhny. He was followed by the rest of the squad and the former Russian president, Boris Yeltsin, who had all but knocked his wife out of the way when he clambered over the front of the VIP box to stride, beaming, onto the court.

Youzhny was being tossed up and down like a rag doll by the time Yeltsin arrived on court. The Russians were in a state of delirious shock, unable to believe they had achieved what no country since 1964—and only three in the history of the event—had done, coming from two rubbers to one down to win the final. In 1964, Australia, in the shape of Fred Stolle (who beat Denis Ralston in five sets) and Roy Emerson, beating the late Chuck McKinley in four, did the honors for the United States.

Marat Safin, never one to be lost for words, described the experience as "better than sex." What more could one add to that.

ABOVE: Yevgeny Kafelnikov **(LEFT)** finally gets his hands on the Davis Cup trophy. Russian hero Mikhail Youzhny is congratulated by Boris Yeltsin **(RIGHT)**.

OPPOSITE: The victorious Russian Davis Cup squad.

PROFILE: MIKHAIL YOUZHNY

BORN | JUNE 25, 1982, IN MOSCOW, RUSSIA

TURNED PROFESSIONAL | 1999

DAVIS CUP RECORDS | SINGLES 2–4 | DOUBLES 0–0

SOMEWHERE IN THEIR DUSTY PHOTOGRAPHIC ANNALS, Jim Courier, Pete Sampras, and Todd Martin may one day come across a memento of the 1995 Davis Cup victory in Moscow, a defining moment in their careers, and wonder if they recognize the young ball boy pictured smiling next to them.

Mikhail Youzhny was the kid muscling in, eager to be pictured with three such notable superstars of the sport. He was one of the crew used in the Russian capital (his birthplace) that year, and no doubt the event left a lasting impression on him.

Enough to go back to work with Boris Sobkin, who had been coaching him since he was ten, and rededicate himself to the sport in which he had already shown enough promise to be marked down as one of Russia's leading prospects. He had first picked up a racket at the age of six, following his older brother, Andrei, into the sport. His hero at the time was Stefan Edberg, arguably the most graceful player ever to become the world's number one.

Youzhny, in his ball boy gear, watched with fascination as Sampras ran himself into the ground to win the Cup for the United States. Mikhail became an outstanding junior player himself, reaching the final of the Australian Open in 1999, where he lost to Kristian Pless of Denmark. Also that year, he won four ITF Futures tournaments, two of them without dropping a set. He was on his way.

He made his debut in Davis Cup in 2000, contesting a dead rubber against Belgium in the first round, when he defeated Olivier Rochus. By 2001, he had edged into the top 100 for the first time, the third youngest player to achieve the feat behind Andy Roddick and Jose Acasuso. His backhand has always been his picture shot, a single-handed feature that has the element of brilliant disguise, a feature that has secured him two fourth-round appearances at Wimbledon, in 2001 and 2002, when he was one of Lleyton Hewitt's victims.

A tragedy befell Mikhail in September last year when his father, also Mikhail, passed away. However, Youzhny went on to reach the final of St. Petersburg, claiming such notable scalps as Andrei Pavel and Younes El Aynaoui. Those performances—and his composed, classic style— prompted the decision of Russian captain Shamil Tarpischev to call upon Youzhny for the final rubber against France and, even when he was two sets to love down, to keep believing in him.

His performance in the final was best summed up by his teammate, Marat Safin. "Of course nobody expected that he could win from two-love down. He surprised I think even himself. He showed that he's a real man, he's a Russian man, he knows how to fight, he knows how to come out of such a difficult situation. Thanks a lot for the victory."

WORLD GROUP

First Round   8-10 February

France defeated Netherlands 3-2, Metz FRA; Clay (I):
Sebastien Grosjean (FRA) d. Edwin Kempes (NED) 75 76(5) 62; Arnaud Clement (FRA) d. Sjeng Schalken (NED) 75 26 67(7) 64 62; Paul Haarhuis/ Sjeng Schalken (NED) d. Cedric Pioline/Fabrice Santoro (FRA) 64 46 61 75; Sebastien Grosjean (FRA) d. Sjeng Schalken (NED) 62 16 76(6) 26 63; Edwin Kempes (NED) d. Arnaud Clement (FRA) 76(5) 63.

Czech Republic defeated Brazil 4-1, Ostrava CZE, Carpet (I):
Jiri Novak (CZE) d. Andre Sa (BRA) 67(10) 61 61 64; Bohdan Ulihrach (CZE) d. Fernando Meligeni (BRA) 63 64 64; Jiri Novak/ David Rikl (CZE) d. Andre Sa/Alexandre Simoni (BRA) 64 63 75; Flavio Saretta (BRA) d. Jan Vacek (CZE) 61 76(6); Bohdan Ulihrach (CZE) d. Andre Sa (BRA) 61 62.

Spain defeated Morocco 3-2, Zaragoza ESP; Clay (I):
Juan Carlos Ferrero (ESP) d. Hicham Arazi (MAR) 63 61 62; Younes El Aynaoui (MAR) d. Alex Corretja (ESP) 63 75 64; Juan Balcells/ Alex Corretja (ESP) d. Karim Alami/Hicham Arazi (MAR) 26 62 76(8) 64; Younes El Aynaoui (MAR) d. Juan Carlos Ferrero (ESP) 76(2) 60 36 06 63; Alex Corretja (ESP) d. Karim Alami (MAR) 63 60 ret.

USA defeated Slovak Republic 5-0, Oklahoma City USA; Hard (I):
Pete Sampras (USA) d. Karol Beck (SVK) 63 67(3) 61 75; Andy Roddick (USA) d. Jan Kroslak (SVK) 64 64 67(5) 76(1); James Blake/Mardy Fish (USA) d. Karol Beck/Jan Kroslak (SVK) 63 67(5) 63 64; James Blake (USA) d. Ladislav Svarc (SVK) 46 63 60; Andy Roddick (USA) d. Karol Beck (SVK) 64 76(5).

Russia defeated Switzerland 3-2, Moscow RUS; Clay (I):
Roger Federer (SUI) d. Marat Safin (RUS) 75 61 62; Yevgeny Kafelnikov (RUS) d. Michel Kratochvil (SUI) 63 46 16 76(3) 62; Yevgeny Kafelnikov/Marat Safin (RUS) d. Roger Federer/Marc Rosset (SUI) 62 76(6) 67(0) 62; Roger Federer (SUI) d. Yevgeny Kafelnikov (RUS) 76(6) 61 61; Marat Safin (RUS) d. Michel Kratochvil (SUI) 61 76(6) 64.

Sweden defeated Great Britain 3-2, Birmingham GBR; Carpet (I):
Tim Henman (GBR) d. Jonas Bjorkman (SWE) 64 75 46 75; Thomas Enqvist (SWE) d. Greg Rusedski (GBR) 76(3) 76(5) 62; Tim Henman/Greg Rusedski (GBR) d. Jonas Bjorkman/Thomas Johansson (SWE) 76(1) 26 67(4) 63 63; Thomas Enqvist (SWE) d. Tim Henman (GBR) 64 62 64; Thomas Johansson (SWE) d. Greg Rusedski (GBR) 46 63 75 64.

Croatia defeated Germany 4-1, Zagreb CRO; Carpet (I):
Rainer Schuettler (GER) d. Ivan Ljubicic (CRO) 57 76(3) 63 76(5); Goran Ivanisevic (CRO) d. Nicolas Kiefer (GER) 76(3) 63 64; Goran Ivanisevic/Ivan Ljubicic (CRO) d. Michael Kohlmann/David Prinosil (GER) 64 64 75; Goran Ivanisevic (CRO) d. Rainer Schuettler (GER) 64 76(4) 76(5); Ivan Ljubicic (CRO) d. Nicolas Kiefer (GER) 76(1) 64.

Argentina defeated Australia 5-0, Buenos Aires ARG; Clay (O):
Guillermo Canas (ARG) d. Scott Draper (AUS) 64 67(4) 57 64 61; Gaston Gaudio (ARG) d. Andrew Ilie (AUS) 61 61 62; Lucas Arnold/Guillermo Canas (ARG) d. Wayne Arthurs/Todd Woodbridge (AUS) 36 63 64 16 108; Juan Ignacio Chela (ARG) d. Andrew Ilie (AUS) 61 61; Gaston Gaudio (ARG) d. Scott Draper (AUS) 63 62.

Quarterfinals   5-7 April

France defeated Czech Republic 3-2, Pau FRA; Carpet (I):
Sebastien Grosjean (FRA) d. Bohdan Ulihrach (CZE) 63 36 06 63 61; Jiri Novak (CZE) d. Nicolas Escude (FRA) 76(4) 61 67(5) 75; Michael Llodra/Fabrice Santoro (FRA) d. Jiri Novak/David Rikl (CZE) 63 61 64; Jiri Novak (CZE) d. Sebastien Grosjean (FRA) 36 61 63 61; Fabrice Santoro (FRA) d. Bohdan Ulihrach (CZE) 76(2) 75 36 46 63.

USA defeated Spain 3-1, Houston USA; Grass (O):
Andy Roddick (USA) d. Tommy Robredo (ESP) 63 75 76(7); Alex Corretja (ESP) d. Pete Sampras (USA) 46 76(4) 75 64; James Blake/Todd Martin (USA) d. Juan Balcells/Alberto Martin (ESP) 61 64 64; Andy Roddick (USA) d. Alberto Martin (ESP) 62 64 62; Tommy Robredo (ESP) led James Blake (USA) 61 54 - play abandoned due to rain.

Russia defeated Sweden 4-1, Moscow RUS; Clay (I):
Marat Safin (RUS) d. Thomas Johansson (SWE) 64 64 64; Yevgeny Kafelnikov (RUS) d. Thomas Enqvist (SWE) 76(6) 63 61; Yevgeny Kafelnikov/Marat Safin (RUS) d. Jonas Bjorkman/Thomas Johansson (SWE) 36 76(6) 67(2) 75 63; Thomas Johansson (SWE) d. Mikhail Youzhny (RUS) 63 64; Andrei Stoliarov (RUS) d. Andreas Vinciguerra (SWE) 46 52 ret.

Argentina defeated Croatia 3-2, Buenos Aires ARG; Clay (O):
Gaston Gaudio (ARG) d. Ivan Ljubicic (CRO) 76(5) 62 63; Juan Ignacio Chela (ARG) d. Ivo Karlovic (CRO) 57 64 64 62; Goran Ivanisevic/Ivan Ljubicic (CRO) d. Lucas Arnold/Guillermo Canas (ARG) 46 26 63 60 86; Ivan Ljubicic (CRO) d. Juan Ignacio Chela (ARG) 63 16 76(5) 64; Gaston Gaudio (ARG) d. Ivo Karlovic (CRO) 64 64 62.

Semifinals   20-22 September

France defeated USA 3-2, Paris FRA; Clay (O):
Arnaud Clement (FRA) d. Andy Roddick (USA) 46 76(6) 76(5) 61; Sebastien Grosjean (FRA) d. James Blake (USA) 64 61 67(7) 75; James Blake/Todd Martin (USA) d. Michael Llodra/Fabrice Santoro (FRA) 26 76(2) 26 64 64; Sebastien Grosjean (FRA) d. Andy Roddick (USA) 64 36 63 64; James Blake (USA) d. Arnaud Clement (FRA) 64 63.

Russia defeated Argentina 3-2, Moscow RUS; Carpet (I):
Marat Safin (RUS) d. Juan Ignacio Chela (ARG) 67(1) 75 75 61; Yevgeny Kafelnikov (RUS) d. Gaston Gaudio (ARG) 36 75 63 26 86; Lucas Arnold/ David Nalbandian (ARG) d. Yevgeny Kafelnikov/ Marat Safin (RUS) 64 64 57 36 1917; Marat Safin (RUS) d. David Nalbandian (ARG) 76(3) 67(5) 60 63; Juan Ignacio Chela (ARG) d. Mikhail Youzhny (RUS) 76(5) 67(3) 64.

Final   29 November – 1 December

Russia defeated France 3-2, Paris FRA; Clay (I):
Marat Safin (RUS) d. Paul-Henri Mathieu (FRA) 64 36 61 64; Sebastien Grosjean (FRA) d. Yevgeny Kafelnikov (RUS) 76(3) 63 60; Nicolas Escude/ Fabrice Santoro (FRA) d. Yevgeny Kafelnikov/Marat Safin (RUS) 63 36 57 63 64; Marat Safin (RUS) d. Sebastien Grosjean (FRA) 63 62 76(11); Mikhail Youzhny (RUS) d. Paul-Henri Mathieu (FRA) 36 26 63 75 64.

World Group Qualifying Round
20-22 September

Australia defeated India 5-0, Adelaide AUS; Hard (O):
Lleyton Hewitt (AUS) d. Harsh Mankad (IND) 61 76(2) 61; Wayne Arthurs (AUS) d. Leander Paes (IND) 64 36 63 64; Lleyton Hewitt/ Todd Woodbridge (AUS) d. Leander Paes/Vishal Uppal (IND) 63 76(5) 61; Scott Draper (AUS) d. Rohan Bopanna (IND) 63 75; Wayne Arthurs (AUS) d. Harsh Mankad (IND) 64 36 75.

Belgium defeated Zimbabwe 4-1, Harare ZIM; Hard (I):
Xavier Malisse (BEL) d. Wayne Black (ZIM) 76(1) 67(3) 75 63; Olivier Rochus (BEL) d. Byron Black (ZIM) 67(4) 64 62 63; Wayne Black/Kevin Ullyett (ZIM) d. Gilles Elseneer/Tom Vanhoudt (BEL) 61 26 76(6) 63; Xavier Malisse (BEL) d. Byron Black (ZIM) 63 76(3) 64; Gilles Elseneer (BEL) d. Genius Chidzikwe (ZIM) 61 64.

Brazil defeated Canada 4-0, Rio de Janeiro BRA; Clay (O):
Fernando Meligeni (BRA) d. Frank Dancevic (CAN) 62 75 26 75; Gustavo Kuerten (BRA) d. Daniel Nestor (CAN) 64 76(10) 60; Gustavo Kuerten/Andre Sa (BRA) d. Simon Larose/Daniel Nestor (CAN) 46 76(5) 61 46 62; Andre Sa (BRA) d. Frank Dancevic (CAN) 63 62; Fernando Meligeni (BRA) v Simon Larose (CAN) - match abandoned due to rain.

Germany defeated Venezuela 5-0, Karlsruhe GER; Hard (I):
Rainer Schuettler (GER) d. Jose de Armas (VEN) 61 61 61; Tommy Haas (GER) d. Jimy Szymanski (VEN) 61 62 61; Nicolas Kiefer/ David Prinosil (GER) d. Jose de Armas/Jimy Szymanski (VEN) 61 63 60; Nicolas Kiefer (GER) d. Kepler Orellana (VEN) 61 75; Rainer Schuettler (GER) d. Jimy Szymanski (VEN) 63 60.

Great Britain defeated Thailand 3-2, Birmingham GBR; Carpet (I):
Tim Henman (GBR) d. Danai Udomchoke (THA) 46 63 62 62; Paradorn Srichaphan (THA) d. Martin Lee (GBR) 60 76(2) 62; Tim Henman/Miles Maclagan (GBR) d. Paradorn Srichaphan/Danai Udomchoke (THA) 67(4) 64 75 62; Tim Henman (GBR) d. Paradorn Srichaphan (THA) 63 62 63; Danai Udomchoke (THA) d. Arvind Parmar (GBR) 63 61.

Netherlands defeated Finland 4-1, Turku FIN; Hard (I):
Raemon Sluiter (NED) d. Jarkko Nieminen (FIN) 46 76(3) 60 76(8); Sjeng Schalken (NED) d. Tuomas Ketola (FIN) 76(13) 63 63; Paul Haarhuis/Sjeng Schalken (NED) d. Tuomas Ketola/Jarkko Nieminen (FIN) 61 64 64; Jarkko Nieminen (FIN) d. Martin Verkerk (NED) 62 64; Raemon Sluiter (NED) d. Timo Nieminen (FIN) 60 63.

Romania defeated Slovak Republic 4-1, Presov SVK; Carpet (I):
Dominik Hrbaty (SVK) d. Adrian Voinea (ROM) 63 64 36 63; Andrei Pavel (ROM) d. Karol Kucera (SVK) 60 63 67(3) 62; Andrei Pavel/Gabriel Trifu (ROM) d. Karol Beck/Dominik Hrbaty (SVK) 67(4) 76(5) 46 63 86; Andrei Pavel (ROM) d. Dominik Hrbaty (SVK) 76(1) 62 62; Victor Hanescu (ROM) d. Karol Beck (SVK) 64 76(1).

Switzerland defeated Morocco 3-2, Casablanca MAR; Clay (O):
Younes El Aynaoui (MAR) d. Michel Kratochvil (SUI) 75 62 62; Roger Federer (SUI) d. Hicham Arazi (MAR) 63 62 61; George Bastl/Roger Federer (SUI) d. Karim Alami/Younes El Aynaoui (MAR) 64 61 64; Roger Federer (SUI) d. Younes El Aynaoui (MAR) 63 62 61; Mounir El Aarej (MAR) d. Michel Kratochvil (SUI) 62 63.

GROUP I

Euro/African Zone
First Round   8-10 February

Zimbabwe defeated Portugal 5-0, Harare ZIM; Hard (I):
Byron Black (ZIM) d. Emanuel Couto (POR) 63 76(4) 75; Wayne Black (ZIM) d. Bernardo Mota (POR) 61 36 63 62; Wayne Black/Kevin Ullyett (ZIM) d. Emanuel Couto/Nuno Marques (POR) 64 64 64; Wayne Black (ZIM) d. Helder Lopes (POR) 76(5) 63; Genius Chidzikwe (ZIM) d. Bernardo Mota (POR) 36 76(6) 75.

Austria defeated Israel 3-2, St Anton-Tirol AUT; Clay (I):
Stefan Koubek (AUT) d. Amir Hadad (ISR) 61 63 76(2); Markus Hipfl (AUT) d. Noam Okun (ISR) 63 46 63 61; Jonathan Erlich/Andy Ram (ISR) d. Alexander Peya/Clemens Trimmel (AUT) 26 64 57 76(5) 62; Stefan Koubek (AUT) d. Noam Okun (ISR) 63 75 64; Amir Hadad (ISR) d. Markus Hipfl (AUT) 63 30 ret.

2nd Round   5-7 April

Finland defeated Italy 4-1, Reggio Calabria ITA; Clay (O):
Kim Tiilikainen (FIN) d. Davide Sanguinetti (ITA) 26 57 63 62 75; Jarkko Nieminen (FIN) d. Giorgio Galimberti (ITA) 63 62 62; Lauri Kiiski/Jarkko Nieminen (FIN) d. Giorgio Galimberti/Mose Navarra (ITA) 63 76(10) 63; Mose Navarra (ITA) d. Timo Nieminen (FIN) 63 75; Kim Tiilikainen (FIN) d. Stefano Galvani (ITA) 63 61.

Zimbabwe defeated Belarus 4-1, Harare ZIM; Hard (I):
Vladimir Voltchkov (BLR) d. Byron Black (ZIM) 76(4) 63 64; Wayne Black (ZIM) d. Max Mirnyi (BLR) 76(3) 63 46 64; Wayne Black/Kevin Ullyett (ZIM) d. Max Mirnyi/Vladimir Voltchkov (BLR) 63 76(4) 46 76(12); Byron Black (ZIM) d. Max Mirnyi (BLR) 63 75 67(3) 63; Genius Chidzikwe (ZIM) d. Alexander Skrypko (BLR) 63 67(5) 63.

Romania defeated Austria 5-0, Constanta ROM; Carpet (I):
Andrei Pavel (ROM) d. Jurgen Melzer (AUT) 61 62 64; Adrian Voinea (ROM) d. Stefan Koubek (AUT) 36 75 63 61; Andrei Pavel/Gabriel Trifu (ROM) d. Julian Knowle/Jurgen Melzer (AUT) 36 61 64 67(6) 62; Andrei Pavel (ROM) d. Alexander Peya (AUT) 61 76(9); Victor Hanescu (ROM) d. Jurgen Melzer (AUT) 64 64.

Belgium defeated Greece 5-0, Liege BEL; Carpet (I):
Xavier Malisse (BEL) d. Nikos Rovas (GRE) 60 76(4) 60; Olivier Rochus (BEL) d. Konstantinos Economidis (GRE) 76(4) 63 61; Gilles Elseneer/Tom Van Houdt (BEL) d. Konstantinos Economidis/Anastasios Vasiliadis (GRE) 67(4) 76(4) 76(1) 64; Gilles Elseneer (BEL) d. Anastasios Vasiliadis (GRE) 62 62; Olivier Rochus (BEL) d. Nikos Rovas (GRE) 75 63.

Finland, Zimbabwe, Romania and Belgium progress to World Group Qualifying Round.

Second Round/Playoff   12-14 July

Belarus defeated Portugal 4-1, Minsk BLR; Carpet (I):
Vladimir Voltchkov (BLR) d. Bernardo Mota (POR) 62 61 62; Max Mirnyi (BLR) d. Helder Lopes (POR) 63 63 64; Max Mirnyi/Vladimir Voltchkov (BLR) d. Nuno Marques/Bernardo Mota (POR) 63 60 63; Alexander Shvec (BLR) d. Leonardo Tavares (POR) 62 76(4); Helder Lopes (POR) d. Alexander Skrypko (BLR) 26 63 64.

Third Round/Playoff   20-22 September

Israel defeated Greece 5-0, Ramat Hasharon ISR; Hard (O):
Harel Levy (ISR) d. Elfterios Alexiou (GRE) 63 61 62; Noam Okun (ISR) d. Alexander Jakupovic (GRE) 63 64 62; Jonathan Erlich/Amir Hadad (ISR) d. Alexander Jakupovic/Nikos Karagiannis (GRE) 75 64 62; Amir Hadad (ISR) d. Elfterios Alexiou (GRE) 60 60 Harel Levy (ISR) d. Nikos Karagiannis (GRE) 64 63.

Italy defeated Portugal 4-1, Follonica ITA; Carpet (I):
Bernardo Mota (POR) d. Stefano Galvani (ITA) 75 63 76(2); Davide Sanguinetti (ITA) d. Leonardo Tavares (POR) 63 62 61; Massimo Bertolini/Giorgio Galimberti (ITA) d. Helder Lopes/Bernardo Mota (POR) 63 67(4) 63 64; Davide Sanguinetti (ITA) d. Bernardo Mota (POR) 64 75 64; Stefano Galvani (ITA) d. Tiago Godinho (POR) 64 61.

Greece and Portugal relegated to Euro/African Zone Group II in 2003.

American Zone
First Round   8-10 February

Venezuela defeated Bahamas 3-2, Nassau BAH; Hard (O):
Jose de Armas (VEN) d. Mark Merklein (BAH) 64 36 62 63; Mark Knowles (BAH) d. Jimy Szymanski (VEN) 61 63 63; Mark Knowles/Mark Merklein (BAH) d. Jose de Armas/Jimy Szymanski (VEN) 26 63 64 64; Jose de Armas (VEN) d. Mark Knowles (BAH) 63 57 63 76(3); Jimy Szymanski (VEN) d. Mark Merklein (BAH) 64 63 61.

Canada defeated Mexico 4-1, Ontario CAN; Carpet (I):
Frederic Niemeyer (CAN) d. Alejandro Hernandez (MEX) 57 63 64 75; Daniel Nestor (CAN) d. Miguel Gallardo (MEX) 63 64 60; Daniel Nestor/Frederic Niemeyer (CAN) d. Santiago Gonzalez/Alejandro Hernandez (MEX) 61 61 61; Miguel Gallardo (MEX) d. Frank Dancevic (CAN) 63 60; Simon Larose (CAN) d. Santiago Gonzalez (MEX) 67(5) 62 62.

Second Round   5-7 April

Venezuela defeated Ecuador 3-2, Lara VEN; Hard (O):
Jose de Armas (VEN) d. Luis Morejon (ECU) 64 63 46 62; Nicolas Lapentti (ECU) d. Jimy Szymanski (VEN) 36 63 75 36 64; Jose de Armas/Jimy Szymanski (VEN) d. Giovanni Lapentti/Nicolas Lapentti 75 62 76(7); Nicolas Lapentti (ECU) d. Jose de Armas (VEN) 61 63 67(5) 46 63; Jimy Szymanski (VEN) d. Luis Morejon (ECU) 46 63 63 62.

Canada defeated Chile 5-0, Calgary CAN; Carpet (I):
Daniel Nestor (CAN) d. Marcelo Rios (CHI) 76(1) 67(2) 63 16 75; Frederic Niemeyer (CAN) d. Fernando Gonzalez (CHI) 67(2) 76(2) 46 63 64; Daniel Nestor/Frederic Niemeyer (CAN) d. Fernando Gonzalez/Hermes Gamonal (CHI) 63 60 62; Frank Dancevic (CAN) d. Guillermo Hormazabal (CHI) 61 64; Simon Larose (CAN) d. Hermes Gamonal (CHI) 63 76(5).

Venezuela and Canada progress to World Group Qualifying Round.

Second Round/Playoff   12-14 July

Ecuador defeated Bahamas 5-0, Guayaquil ECU; Clay (O):
Jhony De Leon (ECU) d. Dentry Mortimer (BAH) 63 61 61; Luis Morejon (ECU) d. Lavaughn Munroe (BAH) 63 63 60; Carlos Avellan/Luis Morejon (ECU) d. Devin Mullings/Patrick-Bjorn Munroe (BAH) 62 63 62; Carlos Avellan (ECU) d. Patrick Munroe (BAH) 61 76(6) Martin Stiegwardt (ECU) d. Devin Mullings (BAH) 36 61 61.

Chile defeated Mexico 3-2, Queretaro Qro MEX; Hard (I):
Nicolas Massu (CHI) d. Alejandro Hernandez (MEX) 63 61 60; Marcelo Rios (CHI) d. Marcelo Amador (MEX) 75 67(3) 63 62; Bruno Echagaray/Santiago Gonzalez (MEX) d. Nicolas Massu/Marcelo Rios (CHI) 63 36 63 62; Alejandro Hernandez (MEX) d. Marcelo Rios (CHI) 76(5) 36 26 60 62; Nicolas Massu (CHI) d. Marcelo Amador (MEX) 63 64 64.

Third Round/Playoff   20-22 September

Bahamas defeated Mexico 3-2, Nassau BAH; Hard (I):
Miguel Gallardo Valles (MEX) d. Mark Merklein (BAH) 57 60 64 76(5); Mark Knowles (BAH) d. Alejandro Hernandez (MEX) 67(4) 62 16 61 64; Mark Knowles/Mark Merklein (BAH) d. Bruno Echagaray/Alejandro Hernandez (MEX) 63 64 62; Miguel Gallardo Valles (MEX) d. Mark Knowles (BAH) 76(6) 36 61 10 ret.; Mark Merklein (BAH) d. Alejandro Hernandez (MEX) 62 63 64.

Mexico relegated to American Zone Group II in 2003.

Asia/Oceania Zone
First Round   8-10 February

Thailand defeated Uzbekistan 3-2, Bangkok THA; Hard (I):
Danai Udomchoke (THA) d. Oleg Ogorodov (UZB) 63 57 62 46 63; Paradorn Srichaphan (THA) d. Vadim Kutsenko (UZB) 64 46 62 46 63; Vadim Kutsenko/Oleg Ogorodov (UZB) d. Vittaya Samrej/Narathorn Srichaphan (THA) 67(3) 64 64 64; Paradorn Srichaphan (THA) d. Oleg Ogorodov (UZB) 76(0) 26 16 75 64; Vadim Kutsenko (UZB) d. Narathorn Srichaphan (THA) 64 67(3) 61.

Japan defeated Korea 3-2, Gunsan, KOR; Carpet (I):
Takao Suzuki (JPN) d. Yong-Il Yoon (KOR) 75 64 63; Hyung-Taik Lee (KOR) d. Gouichi Motomura (JPN) 63 64 61; Hee-Seok Chung/Hyung-Taik Lee (KOR) d. Thomas Shimada/Takao Suzuki (JPN) 64 67(3) 36 75 61; Takao Suzuki (JPN) d. Hyung-Taik Lee (KOR) 76(4) 75 61; Gouichi Motomura (JPN) d. Yong-Il Yoon (KOR) 36 62 62 63.

New Zealand defeated Indonesia 3-2, Invercargill NZL; Carpet (I):
Peter Handoyo (INA) d. Mark Nielsen (NZL) 26 75 63 64; Alistair Hunt (NZL) d. Suwandi (INA) 46 75 46 62 63; Alistair Hunt/ Mark Nielsen (NZL) d. Hendri Susilo Pramono/Febi Widhiyanto (INA) 61 64 36 64; Mark Nielsen (NZL) d. Suwandi (INA) 61 64 36 63; Peter Handoyo (INA) d. Daniel Willman (NZL) 75 63.

India defeated Lebanon 5-0, Beirut LIB; Hard (I):
Leander Paes (IND) d. Karim Alayli (LIB) 63 60 60; Harsh Mankad (IND) d. Ali Hamadeh (LIB) 63 61 61; Mahesh Bhupathi/Leander Paes (IND) d. Patrick Chucri/Ali Hamadeh (LIB) 62 61 63; Leander Paes (IND) d. Patrick Chucri (LIB) 62 62; Harsh Mankad (IND) d. Karim Alayli (LIB) 63 61.

Second Round   5-7 April

Thailand defeated Japan 4-1, Bangkok THA; Hard (O):
Goichi Motomura (JPN) d. Paradorn Srichaphan (THA) 63 76(3) 61; Danai Udomchoke (THA) d. Takao Suzuki (JPN) 62 36 75 52 ret.; Vittaya Samrej/Narathorn Srichaphan (THA) d. Thomas Shimada/Takahiro Terachi (JPN) 16 26 64 32 ret.; Paradorn Srichaphan (THA) d. Takao Suzuki (JPN) 62 64 62; Danai Udomchoke (THA) d. Goichi Motomura (JPN) 75 62.

India defeated New Zealand 4-1, Wellington, NZL; Hard (O):
Mark Nielsen (NZL) d. Harsh Mankad (IND) 64 60 61; Leander Paes (IND) d. Alistair Hunt (NZL) 63 64 64; Mahesh Bhupathi/ Leander Paes (IND) d. James Shortall/Daniel Willman (NZL) 64 63 64; Leander Paes (IND) d. Mark Nielsen (NZL) 64 63 46 26 61; Harsh Mankad (IND) d. James Shortall (NZL) 75 63.

Thailand and India progress to World Group Qualifying Round.

Second Round/Playoff   5-7 April

Uzbekistan defeated Korea 4-1, Tashkent UZB; Hard (I):
Hee-Seok Chung (KOR) d. Vadim Kutsenko (UZB) 62 64 46 61; Oleg Ogorodov (UZB) d. Seung-Bok Baek (KOR) 61 63 61; Vadim Kutsenko/Oleg Ogorodov (UZB) d. Hee-Seok Chung/Dong-Hyun Kim (KOR) 64 36 62 46 63; Oleg Ogorodov (UZB) d. Hee-Seok Chung (KOR) 67(2) 64 60 62; Vadim Kutsenko (UZB) d. Seung-Bok Baek (KOR) 76(4) 64.

Indonesia defeated Lebanon 4-1, Surabaya INA; Hard (O):
Suwandi Suwandi (INA) d. Patrick Chucri (LIB) 62 62 64; Febi Widhiyanto (INA) d. Ali Hamadeh (LIB) 64 61 60; Hendri-Susilo Pramono/Bonit Wiryawan (INA) d. Patrick Chucri/Ali Hamadeh (LIB) 75 76(7) 64; Suwandi Suwandi (INA) d. Fady Youssef (LIB) 60 60; Patrick Chucri (LIB) d. Febi Widhiyanto (INA) 62 76(5).

Third Round/Playoff   20-22 September

Korea defeated Lebanon 5-0, Jounieh LIB; Clay (O):
Dong-Hyun Kim (KOR) d. Sean Karam (LIB) 61 61 61; Hee-Seok Chung (KOR) d. Karim Alayli (LIB) 62 61 63; Hee-Seok Chung/Hee-Sung Chung (KOR) d. Patrick Chucri/Sean Karam (LIB) 62 62 62; Dong-Hyun Kim (KOR) d. Karim Alayli (LIB) 76(1) 61; Oh-Hee Kwon (KOR) d. Patrick Chucri (LIB) 63 63.

Lebanon relegated to Asia/Oceania Zone Group II in 2003.

GROUP II

Euro/African Zone
First Round   3-5 May

Bulgaria defeated Ukraine 3-2, Odesa UKR; Clay (O):
Orest Tereshchuk (UKR) d. Milen Velev (BUL) 63 26 64 61; Todor Enev (BUL) d. Andrey Dernovskiy (UKR) 64 61 63; Todor Enev/ Milen Velev (BUL) d. Andrey Dernovskiy/Orest Tereshchuk (UKR) 76(5) 67(5) 76(4) 63; Orest Tereshchuk (UKR) d. Todor Enev (BUL) 63 76(1) 36 64; Milen Velev (BUL) d. Andrey Dernovskiy (UKR) 75 57 64 63.

Denmark defeated Moldova 5-0, Chisinau MDA; Clay (O):
Kenneth Carlsen (DEN) d. Andrei Gorban (MDA) 60 61 63; Patrik Langvardt (DEN) d. Evghenii Plugariov (MDA) 64 64 75; Kenneth Carlsen/Patrik Langvardt (DEN) d. Andrei Gorban/Victor Ribas (MDA) 61 60 64; Kasper Warming (DEN) d. Evghenii Plugariov (MDA) 64 64; Mik Ledvonova (DEN) d. Andrei Gorban (MDA) 63 61.

Yugoslavia defeated South Africa 3-2, Belgrade YUG; Clay (O):
Vladimir Pavicevic (YUG) d. Justin Bower (RSA) 63 62 57 76(2); Dusan Vemic (YUG) d. Louis Vosloo (RSA) 63 64 36 75(5); Jeff Coetzee/John-Laffnie de Jager (RSA) d. Darko Madjarovski/Dusan Vemic (YUG) 75 64 62; Vladimir Pavicevic (YUG) d. Louis Vosloo (RSA) 63 62 36 76(0); Justin Bower (RSA) d. Vladimir Obradovic (YUG) 75 63.

Ireland defeated Armenia 3-0, Yerevan ARM; Clay (O):
John Doran (IRL) d. Tsolak Gevorgyan (ARM) 64 61 75; Peter Clarke (IRL) d. Hayk Hakobyan (ARM) 60 75 62; Owen Casey/ John Doran (IRL) d. Tsolak Gevorgyan/Harutiun Sofian (ARM) 75 63 64; Tsolak Gevorgyan (ARM) v Peter Clarke (IRL) not played; Hayk Hakobyan (ARM) v John Doran (IRL) not played.

Cote d'Ivoire defeated Latvia 4-1, Liepajas LAT; Clay (O):
Valentin Sanon (CIV) d. Andis Juska (LAT) 62 63 16 46 61; Claude N'Goran (CIV) d. Andris Filimonovs (LAT) 46 75 61 76 (4); Andris Filimonovs/Andis Juska (LAT) d. Ilou Lonfo/Claude N'Goran (CIV) 46 62 63 16 63; Valentin Sanon (CIV) d. Andris Filimonovs (LAT) 63 61 75; Claude N'Goran (CIV) d. Andis Juska (LAT) 63 76(2).

Norway defeated Egypt 4-1, Asker NOR; Clay (O):
Jan Frode Andersen (NOR) d. Amro Ghoneim (EGY) 76(5) 60 62; Stian Boretti (NOR) d. Karim Maamoun (EGY) 57 63 64 64; Jan Frode Andersen/Helge Koll-Frafjord (NOR) d. Amro Ghoneim/ Karim Maamoun (EGY) 26 62 63 62; Helge Koll-Frafjord (NOR) d. Karim Maamoun (EGY) 62 57 64; Mohamed Maamoun (EGY) d. Fredrik Aarum (NOR) 62 76 (4).

Luxembourg defeated Hungary 4-1 Luxembourg LUX; Hard (I):
Mike Scheidweiler (LUX) d. Kornel Bardoczky (HUN) 67(2) 62 62 75; Gilles Muller (LUX) d. Attila Savolt (HUN) 63 76(8) 67(5) 67(2) 63; Gilles Muller/Mike Scheidweiler (LUX) d. Gergely Kisgyorgy/Attila Savolt (HUN) 57 63 36 64 119; Gilles Kremer (LUX) d. Zsolt Tatar (HUN) 67(2) 76(2) 63; Gergely Kisgyorgy (HUN) d. Pascal Schaul (LUX) 64 67(5) 63.

Slovenia defeated Ghana 4-1, Ljubljana SLO; Clay (O):
Iztok Bozic (SLO) d. Gunther Darkey (GHA) 75 46 75 60; Marko Tkalec (SLO) d. Henry Adjei-Darko (GHA) 61 63 75; Marko Tkalec/ Matija Zgaga (SLO) d. Henry Adjei-Darko/Gunther Darkey (GHA) 63 64 26 64; Matija Zgaga (SLO) d. Samuel Fumi (GHA) 63 62; Henry Adjei-Darko (GHA) d. Bostjan Osabnik (SLO) 63 76(1).

Second Round   12-14 July

Cote D'Ivoire defeated Bulgaria 3-2, Abidjan CIV; Hard (O):
Valentin Sanon (CIV) d. Ivo Bratanov (BUL) 62 75 76(6); Todor Enev (BUL) d. Claude N'Goran (CIV) 36 75 67(2) 75 63; Claude N'Goran/Valentin Sanon (CIV) d. Todor Enev/Milen Velev (BUL) 64 57 62 16 64; Todor Enev (BUL) d. Valentin Sanon (CIV) 67(3) 36 61 76(5) 61; Claude N'Goran (CIV) d. Ivo Bratanov (BUL) 62 63 26 46 62.

Norway defeated Denmark 3-2, Hornbaek DEN; Hard (O):
Kenneth Carlsen (DEN) d. Stian Boretti (NOR) 64 64 61; Jan Frode Andersen (NOR) d. Jonathan Printzlau (DEN) 61 64 62; Jan Frode Andersen/Helge Koll-Frafjord (NOR) d. Thomas Andersen/Kenneth Carlsen (DEN) 67(6) 64 64; Kenneth Carlsen (DEN) d. Jan Frode Andersen (NOR) 64 76(4) 26 76(5); Stian Boretti (NOR) d. Patrik Langvardt (DEN) 76(3) 62 76(5).

Luxembourg defeated Yugoslavia 3-2, Esch/Alzette LUX; Hard (O):
Gilles Muller (LUX) d. Nenad Zimonjic (YUG) 62 61 63; Janko Tipsarevic (YUG) d. Mike Scheidweiler (LUX) 64 75 46 64; Vladimir Pavicevic/Nenad Zimonjic (YUG) d. Gilles Muller/Mike Scheidweiler (LUX) 64 16 61 76(7); Mike Scheidweiler (LUX) d. Vladimir Pavicevic (YUG) 63 75 63; Gilles Muller (LUX) d. Janko Tipsarevic (YUG) 46 76(5) 76(4) 64.

Slovenia defeated Ireland 3-2, Portoro SLO; Clay (O):
Marko Tkalec (SLO) d. John Doran (IRL) 76(4) 26 64 76(3); Peter Clarke (IRL) d. Iztok Bozic (SLO) 64 62 62; Peter Clarke/ John Doran (IRL) d. Marko Tkalec/Matija Zgaga (SLO) 76(5) 16 75 62; Marko Tkalec (SLO) d. Peter Clarke (IRL) 46 64 61 61; Iztok Bozic (SLO) d. David Mullins (IRL) 60 62 76(3).

Third Round   20-22 September

Luxembourg defeated Slovenia 3-2, Esch/Alzette LUX; Hard (I):
Mike Scheidweiler (LUX) d. Marko Tkalec (SLO) 61 36 63 75; Gilles Muller (LUX) d. Andrej Kracman (SLO) 76(6) 63 63; Gilles Muller/Mike Scheidweiler (LUX) d. Andrej Kracman/Marko Tkalec (SLO) 62 64 64; Marko Tkalec (SLO) d. Gilles Kremer (LUX) 63 36 63; Andrej Kracman (SLO) d. Mike Scheidweiler (LUX) 64 76(4).

Norway defeated Cote d'Ivoire 4-1, Asker NOR; Clay (O):
Jan Frode Andersen (NOR) d. Valentin Sanon (CIV) 62 63 60; Stian Boretti (NOR) d. Claude N'Goran (CIV) 76(2) 36 63 62; Jan Frode Andersen/Stian Boretti (NOR) d. Claude N'Goran/Valentin Sanon (CIV) 46 62 63 60; Claude N'Goran (CIV) d. Fredrik Aarum (NOR) 36 63 63; Stian Boretti (NOR) d. Valentin Sanon (CIV) 62 60.

Luxembourg and Norway promoted to Euro/African Zone Group II in 2003.

Playoff   12-14 July

Ukraine defeated Latvia 4-1, Jurmala LAT; Clay (O):
Andrey Dernovskiy (**UKR**) d. Andris Filimonovs (**LAT**) 64 64 62;
Orest Tereshchuk (**UKR**) d. Andis Juska (**LAT**) 61 62 62; Orest
Tereshchuk/Sergei Yaroshenko (**UKR**) d. Andris Filimonovs/Andis
Juska (**LAT**) 75 62 62; Sergei Yaroshenko (**UKR**) d. Deniss Pavlovs
(**LAT**) 67(5) 63 64; Andis Juska (**LAT**) d. Andrey Dernovskiy (**UKR**)
63 31 ret.

Egypt defeated Moldova 5-0, Cairo EGY; Clay (O):
Amro Ghoneim (**EGY**) d. Evghenii Plugariov (**MDA**) 26 62 75 60;
Karim Maamoun (**EGY**) d. Andrei Gorban (**MDA**) 60 64 62; Karim
Maamoun/Mohamed Maamoun (**EGY**) d. Serghei Cuptov/Evghenii
Plugariov (**MDA**) 60 63 61; Mohamed Maamoun (**EGY**) d. Alexandru
Andronachi (**MDA**) 60 62; Mohamed Wafa (**EGY**) d. Andrei Gorban
(**MDA**) 26 63 64.

South Africa defeated Hungary 3-2, Pretoria RSA; Hard (O):
Rik de Voest (**RSA**) d. Gergely Kisgyorgy (**HUN**) 63 64 67(2) 76(3);
Wesley Moodie (**RSA**) d. Gabor Jaross (**HUN**) 76(5) 76(4) 62; John-
Laffnie de Jager/Robbie Koenig (**RSA**) d. Gergely Kisgyorgy/Balazs
Veress (**HUN**) 26 62 62 61; Gergely Kisgyorgy (**HUN**) d. Wesley
Moodie (**RSA**) 75 67(5) 76(5); Balazs Veress (**HUN**) d. Rik de Voest
(**RSA**) 61 26 63.

Ghana defeated Armenia 4-1, Accra GHA; Hard (O):
Henry Adjei-Darko (**GHA**) d. Tsolak Gevorgyan (**ARM**) 63 76(2) 63;
Gunther Darkey (**GHA**) d. Harutiun Sofian (**ARM**) 76(0) 60 76(3);
Henry Adjei-Darko/Gunther Darkey (**GHA**) d. Tsolak Gevorgyan/
Harutiun Sofian (**ARM**) 63 62 64; Kwasi Ahenkora (**GHA**) d. Tsolak
Gevorgyan (**ARM**) 63 36 76(6); Harutiun Sofian (**ARM**) d. Fred Eggir
(**GHA**) 64 63.

*Armenia, Hungary, Latvia and Moldova relegated to Euro/African
Zone Group III in 2003.*

American Zone
First Round   8-10 February

Peru defeated Guatemala 4-1, Guatemala City GUA; Hard (O):
Luis Horna (**PER**) d. Rodrigo Gabriel (**GUA**) 60 60 61; Jacobo
Chavez (**GUA**) d. Ivan Miranda (**PER**) 16 26 75 63 64; Luis Horna/
Ivan Miranda (**PER**) d. Jacobo Chavez/Cristian Paiz (**GUA**) 46 63 36
63 75; Luis Horna (**PER**) d. Jacobo Chavez (**GUA**) 63 64 62; Mario
Monroy (**PER**) d. Cristian Paiz (**GUA**) 75 63.

**Paraguay defeated Netherlands Antilles 5-0, Lambare PAR;
Clay (O):**
Francisco Rodriguez (**PAR**) d. Elmar Gerth (**AHO**) 64 61 63; Ramon
Delgado (**PAR**) d. Raoul Behr (**AHO**) 61 60 61; Paulo Carvallo/
Ramon Delgado (**PAR**) d. Piet Hein Boekel/Elmar Gerth (**AHO**) 64
64 62; Emilio Baez-Britez (**PAR**) d. Piet Hein Boekel (**AHO**) 61 61;
Francisco Rodriguez (**PAR**) d. Raoul Behr (**AHO**) 61 62.

Colombia defeated Cuba 5-0, Villavicencio COL; Clay (O):
Pablo Gonzalez (**COL**) d. Lazaro Navarro (**CUB**) 64 75 64; Michael
Quintero (**COL**) d. Ricardo Chile (**CUB**) 63 63 63; Pablo Gonzalez/
Carlos Salamanca (**COL**) d. Sandor Martinez/Lazaro Navarro (**CUB**)
76(6) 76(3) 62; Michael Quintero (**COL**) d. Sandor Martinez (**CUB**)
36 76(5) 62; Pablo Gonzalez (**COL**) d. Ricardo Chile (**CUB**) 60 64.

**Uruguay defeated Trinidad & Tobago 5-0, Port-of-Spain TRI;
Hard (O):**
Martin Vilarrubi (**URU**) d. Shane Stone (**TRI**) 62 62 76(4); Federico
Dondo (**URU**) d. Troy Stone (**TRI**) 64 63 61; Marcelo Barboza/
Marcel Felder (**URU**) d. Shane Stone/Troy Stone (**TRI**) 57 16 75
76(7) 64; Marcel Felder (**URU**) d. Tyler Mayers (**TRI**) 63 60; Martin
Vilarrubi (**URU**) d. Ivor Grazette (**TRI**) 60 60.

Second Round   5-7 April

Peru defeated Paraguay 3-2, Lambare PAR; Clay (O):
Ramon Delgado (**PAR**) d. Ivan Miranda (**PER**) 63 75 64; Luis Horna
(**PER**) d. Francisco Rodriguez (**PAR**) 76(6) 64 62; Luis Horna/Ivan
Miranda (**PER**) d. Paulo Carvallo/Ramon Delgado (**PAR**) 64 76(7)
63; Luis Horna (**PER**) d. Ramon Delgado (**PAR**) 62 76(4) 75;
Francisco Rodriguez (**PAR**) d. Mario Monroy (**PER**) 62 75.

Uruguay defeated Colombia 3-2, Villavicencio COL; Clay (O):
Pablo Gonzalez (**COL**) d. Pablo Bianchi (**URU**) 75 46 60 62;
Federico Dondo (**URU**) d. Michael Quinterro (**COL**) 76(4) 63 64;
Marcelo Barboza/Federico Dondo (**URU**) d. Alejandro Falla/Carlos
Salamanca (**COL**) 06 76(5) 64 64; Alejandro Falla (**COL**) d. Pablo
Bianchi (**URU**) 62 75 75; Federico Dondo (**URU**) d. Pablo Gonzalez
(**COL**) 67(3) 64 61 64.

Final   12-14 July

Peru defeated Uruguay 4-1, Montevideo URU; Clay (O):
Ivan Miranda (**PER**) d. Federico Dondo (**URU**) 61 63 60; Luis Horna
(**PER**) d. Martin Vilarrubi (**URU**) 57 75 62 61; Marcel Felder/Martin
Vilarrubi (**URU**) d. Luis Horna/Ivan Miranda (**PER**) 36 64 62 62;
Luis Horna (**PER**) d. Pablo Bianchi (**URU**) 61 46 61 61; Luis Felipe
Noriega (**PER**) d. Marcel Felder (**URU**) 61 67(2) 76(5).

Peru promoted to American Zone Group I in 2003.

Playoff   5-7 April

**Netherlands Antilles defeated Guatemala 3-2, Guatemala City
GUA; Hard (O):**
Jean-Julien Rojer (**AHO**) d. Luis Perez-Chete (**GUA**) 63 67(4) 63 64;
Jacobo Chavez (**GUA**) d. Elmar Gerth (**AHO**) 61 62 61; Elmar Gerth/
Jean-Julien Rojer (**AHO**) d. Jacobo Chavez/Luis Perez-Chete (**GUA**)
76(5) 36 63 64; Jean-Julien Rojer (**AHO**) d. Jacobo Chavez (**GUA**)
61 64 63; Cristian Paiz (**GUA**) d. Raoul Behr (**AHO**) 62 63.

**Cuba defeated Trinidad & Tobago 5-0, Ciudad de Habana CUB;
Hard (O):**
Ricardo Chile-Fonte (**CUB**) d. Shane Stone (**TRI**) 36 60 64 46 63;
Lazaro Navarro-Batles (**CUB**) d. Ivor Grazette (**TRI**) 62 62 64;
Sandor Martinez-Breijo/Lazaro Navarro-Batles (**CUB**) d. Shane
Stone/Troy Stone (**TRI**) 61 46 63 75; Sandor Martinez-Breijo (**CUB**)
d. Shane Stone (**TRI**) 64 36 64; Yanquiel Medina Sobrino (**CUB**)
d.Troy Stone (**TRI**) 62 20 ret.

*Guatemala and Trinidad & Tobago relegated to American Zone
Group III in 2003.*

Asia/Oceania Zone
First Round   8-10 February

China defeated Kuwait 4-1, Shenzhen CHN; Hard (O):
Ben-Qiang Zhu (**CHN**) d. Mosaad Al-Jazzaf (**KUW**) 60 60 60;
Mohammad Al-Ghareeb (**KUW**) d. Yu Wang (**CHN**) 63 75 64; Ran
Xu/Shao-Xuan Zeng (**CHN**) d. Husain Al-Ashwak/ Mohammad
Al-Ghareeb (**KUW**) 60 63 64; Ben-Qiang Zhu (**CHN**) d. Husain
Al-Ashwak (**KUW**) 61 61 61; Yu Wang (**CHN**) d. Mosaad Al-Jazzaf
(**KUW**) 75 61.

Kazakhstan defeated Philippines 4-1, Almaty KAZ; Hard (I):
Dias Doskarayev (**KAZ**) d. Joseph Victorino (**PHI**) 46 64 63 60;
Alexey Kedrijuk (**KAZ**) d. Johnny Arcilla (**PHI**) 62 62 46 63; Dias
Doskarayev/Alexey Kedrijuk (**KAZ**) d. Adelo Abadia/Johnny Arcilla
(**PHI**) 36 46 63 76(5) 97; Anton Tsymbalov (**KAZ**) d. Joseph
Victorino (**PHI**) 62 36 75; Michael Mora III (**PHI**) d. Dmitriy
Makeyev (**KAZ**) 76(2) 64.

Pakistan defeated Malaysia 4-1, Kuala Lumpur MAS; Hard (I):
Asim Shafik (**PAK**) d. Hazuan Hizan (**MAS**) 63 46 61 64; Aisam-UI-
Haq Qureshi (**PAK**) d. Yew Ming Si (**MAS**) 76(6) 76(2) 67(3) 62;
Aqueel Khan/ Aisam-UI-Haq Qureshi (**PAK**) d. Darmadi Jamal/Yew
Ming Si (**MAS**) 63 62 57 62; Nomi Qamar (**PAK**) d. Adam Jaya 63
62; Yew Ming Si (**MAS**) d. Asim Shafik (**PAK**) 67(10) 76(4) 64.

**Chinese Taipei defeated China Hong Kong 4-1, Hong Kong, HKG;
Hard (O):**
Michael Brown (**HKG**) d. Wei-Jen Cheng (**TPE**) 46 61 76(4) 61;
Yeu-Tzuoo Wang (**TPE**) d. Chris Numbers (**HKG**) 61 62 64; Chia-Che
Liu/Yeu-Tzuoo Wang (**TPE**) d. John Hui/Melvin Tong (**HKG**) 61 62
36 61; Yeu-Tzuoo Wang (**TPE**) d. Michael Brown (**HKG**) 61 36 64
62; Wei-Jen Cheng (**TPE**) d. John Hui (**HKG**) 62 76(5).

Second Round   5-7 April

China, P.R. defeated Kazakhstan 3-2, Wuhan CHN; Hard (O):
Alexey Kedriouk (**KAZ**) d. Yu Wang (**CHN**) 63 62 67(4) 26 60; Dias
Doskaraev (**KAZ**) d. Ben-Qiang Zhu (**CHN**) 26 63 63 64; Ran Xu/
Shao-Xuan Zeng (**CHN**) d. Dias Doskaraev/Alexey Kedriouk (**KAZ**) 64
60 76(1); Ben-Qiang Zhu (**CHN**) d. Alexey Kedriouk (**KAZ**) 36 76(3)
62 46 61; Yu Wang (**CHN**) d. Dias Doskaraev (**KAZ**) 64 63 61.

Pakistan defeated Chinese Taipei 4-1, Lahore PAK; Grass (O):
Aqeel Khan (**PAK**) d. Wei-Jen Cheng (**TPE**) 46 63 63 60; Aisam UI-
Haq Qureshi (**PAK**) d. Wen-Lung Chang (**TPE**) 76(5) 63 ret.; Aqeel
Khan/Aisam UI-Haq Qureshi (**PAK**) d. Chia-Che Liu/Simon Shen
(**TPE**) 64 26 64 64; Aisam UI-Haq Qureshi (**PAK**) d. Wei-Jen Cheng
(**TPE**) 62 61; Simon Shen (**TPE**) d. Asim Shafik (**PAK**) 75 62.

Final 20-22 September

Pakistan defeated China, P.R. 3-2, Peshawar PAK; Grass (O):
Ben Qiang Zhu **(CHN)** d. Aqeel Khan **(PAK)** 61 61 67(5) 76(2); Aisam-Ul-Haq Qureshi **(PAK)** d. Yu Wang **(CHN)** 62 63 62; Aqeel Khan/Aisam-Ul-Haq Qureshi **(PAK)** d. Ran Xu/Shao Xuan Zeng **(CHN)** 67(3) 75 36 76(7) 1210; Ben Qiang Zhu **(CHN)** d. Aisam-Ul-Haq Qureshi **(PAK)** 46 46 63 61 61; Aqeel Khan **(PAK)** d. Yu Wang **(CHN)** 61 64 75.

Pakistan promoted to Asia/Oceania Zone Group I in 2003.

Playoff 5-7 April

Philippines defeated Kuwait 3-2, Manila PHI; Clay (I):
Johnny Arcilla **(PHI)** d. Musaad Al-Jazzaf **(KUW)** 76(4) 57 61 64; Mohammad Al-Ghareeb **(KUW)** d. Adelo Abadia **(PHI)** 75 63 75; Adelo Abadia/Johnny Arcilla **(PHI)** d. Hussain Al-Ashwak/Mohammad Al-Ghareeb **(KUW)** 46 63 76(4) 61; Mohammad Al-Ghareeb **(KUW)** d. Johnny Arcilla **(PHI)** 60 63 62; Adelo Abadia **(PHI)** d. Musaad Al-Jazzaf **(KUW)** 63 62 61.

China Hong Kong defeated Malaysia 5-0, Hong Kong HKG; Hard (I):
Michael Brown **(HKG)** d. Yew Ming Si **(MAS)** 63 64 75; John Hui **(HKG)** d. Hazuan Hizan **(MAS)** 62 63 16 75; John Hui/Melvin Tong **(HKG)** d. Adam Jaya/Yew Ming Si **(MAS)** 36 64 76(3) 63; Hiu Tong Yu **(HKG)** d. Adam Jaya **(MAS)** 57 63 60; Michael Brown **(HKG)** d. Dannio Yahya **(MAS)** 60 75.

Kuwait and Malaysia relegated to Asia/Oceania Zone Group III in 2003.

GROUP III

Euro/African Zone – Venue I

Date: 1-7 April Venue: Antalya, Turkey Surface: Clay (O)
Group A: Andorra, Lithuania, Monaco, Namibia
Group B: Bosnia & Herzegovina, Botswana, Iceland, Turkey

Group A

3 April Monaco defeated Namibia 3-0:
Christophe Bosio **(MON)** d. Henrico du Plessis **(NAM)** 63 36 86; Guillaume Couillard **(MON)** d. Johan Theron **(NAM)** 62 60; Christophe Bosio/Emmanuel Heussner **(MON)** d. Henrico Du Plessis/Johan Theron **(NAM)** 36 64 64.

Andorra defeated Lithuania 2-1:
Alvaras Balzekas **(LTU)** d. Jean Baptiste Poux **(AND)** 62 63; Joan Jimenez Guerra **(AND)** d. Rolandas Murashka **(LTU)** 64 75; Joan Jimenez Guerra/Jean Baptiste Poux **(AND)** d. Rolandas Murashka/Gvidas Sabeckis **(LTU)** 64 76(2).

4 April Lithuania defeated Namibia 3-0:
Alvaras Balzekas **(LTU)** d. Henrico du Plessis **(NAM)** 62 61; Rolandas Murashka **(LTU)** d. Johan Theron **(NAM)** 61 61; Rolandas Murashka/Gvidas Sabeckis **(LTU)** d. Nicky Buys/Jean-Pierre Huish **(NAM)** 64 63.

Monaco defeated Andorra 2-1:
Emmanuel Heussner **(MON)** d. Jean Baptiste Poux **(AND)** 64 63; Joan Jimenez Guerra **(AND)** d. Guillaume Couillard **(MON)** 76(3) 57 64; Christophe Bosio/Emmanuel Heussner **(MON)** d. Joan Jimenez Guerra/Kenneth Tuilier-Curco **(AND)** 75 46 63.

5 April Andorra defeated Namibia 2-1:
Kenneth Tuilier **(AND)** d. Nicky Buys **(NAM)** 61 60; Joan Jimenez Guerra **(AND)** d. Jean-Pierre Huish **(NAM)** 62 60; Henrico du Plessis/Johan Theron **(NAM)** d. Joan Jimenez Guerra/Jean Baptiste Poux **(AND)** 30 ret.

Monaco defeated Lithuania 3-0:
Emmanuel Heussner **(MON)** d. Alvaras Balzekas **(LTU)** 75 36 61; Guillaume Couillard **(MON)** d. Rolandas Murashka **(LTU)** 62 62; Christophe Boggetti/ Christophe Bosio **(MON)** d. Alvaras Balzekas/Gvidas Sabeckis **(LTU)** 75 75.

Group B

3 April Turkey defeated Botswana 3-0:
Haluk Akkoyun **(TUR)** d. Modisaotsile Phatshwane **(BOT)** 62 61; Barish Erguin **(TUR)** d. Petrus Molefe **(BOT)** 6161; Esat Tanik/Ergun Zorlu **(TUR)** d. Petrus Molefe/Uyapo Nleya **(BOT)** 62 60.

Iceland defeated Bosnia & Herzegovina 2-1:
Igor Ibrisbegovic **(BIH)** d. David Halldorsson **(ISL)** 63 61; Arnar Sigurdsson **(ISL)** d. Igor Racic **(BIH)** 64 64; David Halldorsson/ Arnar Sigurdsson **(ISL)** d. Ismar Gorcic/ Igor Ibrisbegovic **(BIH)** 63 75.

4 April Bosnia & Herzegovina defeated Botswana 3-0:
Igor Ibrisbegovic **(BIH)** d. Uyapo Nleya **(BOT)** 60 62; Igor Racic **(BIH)** d. Petrus Molefe **(BOT)** 62 60; Ismar Gorcic/Igor Racic **(BIH)** d. Uyapo Nleya/Modisaotsile Phatshwane (BOT) 60 60.

Turkey defeated Iceland 2-1:
Haluk Akkoyun **(TUR)** d. David Halldorsson **(ISL)** 61 60; Arnar Sigurdsson **(ISL)** d. Barish Erguin **(TUR)** 64 75; Haluk Akkoyun/Barish Erguin **(TUR)** d. David Halldorsson/Arnar Sigurdsson **(ISL)** 64 61.

5 April Bosnia & Herzegovina defeated Turkey 2-1:
Igor Ibrisbegovic **(BIH)** d. Haluk Akkoyun **(TUR)** 63 63; Igor Racic **(BIH)** d. Baris Ergun **(TUR)** 61 67(2) 61; Haluk Akkoyun/Barish Erguin **(TUR)** d. Ismar Gorcic/Igor Ibrisbegovic **(BIH)** 64 46 63.

Iceland defeated Botswana 3-0:
David Halldorsson **(ISL)** d. Modisaotsile Phatshwane **(BOT)** 61 36 64; Arnar Sigurdsson **(ISL)** d. Petrus Molefe **(BOT)** 60 62; David Halldorsson/Arnar Sigurdsson **(ISL)** d. Petrus Molefe/Uyapo Nleya **(BOT)** 62 61.

Playoff for 1st-4th Positions:
Results carried forward:
Monaco defeated Andorra 2-1;
Bosnia & Herzegovina defeated Turkey 2-1.

6 April Andorra defeated Bosnia & Herzegovina 2-1:
Kenneth Tuilier **(AND)** d. Igor Ibrisbegovic **(BIH)** 75 60; Joan Jimenez Guerra **(AND)** d. Igor Racic **(BIH)** 61 61; Ivan Dodig/Igor Racic **(BIH)** d. Joan Jimenez Guerra/Jean Baptiste Poux **(AND)** 63 36 63.

Monaco defeated Turkey 3-0:
Christophe Bosio **(MON)** d. Esat Tanik **(TUR)** 16 76(5) 63; Guillaume Couillard **(MON)** d. Haluk Akkoyun **(TUR)** 62 64; Guillaume Couillard/Emmanuel Heussner **(MON)** d. Barish Erguin/Ergun Zorlu **(TUR)** 64 46 61.

7 April Monaco defeated Bosnia & Herzegovina 3-0:
Emmanuel Heussner **(MON)** d. Igor Ibrisbegovic **(BIH)** 60 ret; Guillaume Couillard **(MON)** d. Igor Racic **(BIH)** 60 63; Christophe Bosio/Emmanuel Heussner **(MON)** d. Ivan Dodig/Igor Racic **(BIH)** 61 61.

Turkey defeated Andorra 2-1:
Esat Tanik **(TUR)** d. Kenneth Tuilier **(AND)** 75 61; Joan Jimenez Guerra **(AND)** d. Barish Erguin **(TUR)** 62 62; Esat Tanik/Ergun Zorlu **(TUR)** d. Oscar Pons/Kenneth Tuilier **(AND)** 62 76(2).

Playoff for 5th-8th Positions:
Results carried forward:
Lithuania defeated Namibia 3-0;
Iceland defeated Botswana 3-0.

6 April Lithuania defeated Botswana 3-0:
Gvidas Sabeckis **(LTU)** d. Uyapo Nleya **(BOT)** 61 62; Alvaras Balzekas **(LTU)** d. Modisaotsile Phatshwane **(BOT)** 60 61; Rolandas Murashka/Gvidas Sabeckis **(LTU)** d. Uyapo Nleya/Modisaotsile Phatshwane **(BOT)** 63 61.

Namibia defeated Iceland 2-1:
Henrico du Plessis **(NAM)** d. Andri Jonsson **(ISL)** 61 60; Arnar Sigurdsson **(ISL)** d. Johan Theron **(NAM)** 63 36 75; Henrico du Plessis/Johan Theron **(NAM)** d. David Halldorsson/Arnar Sigurdsson **(ISL)** 63 46 64.

7 April Namibia defeated Botswana 3-0:
Henrico du Plessis **(NAM)** d. Uyapo Nleya **(BOT)** 60 60; Johan Theron **(NAM)** d. Modisaotsile Phatshwane **(BOT)** 60 60; Nicky Buys/Jean-Pierre Huish **(NAM)** d. Moses Motate/Modisaotsile Phatshwane **(BOT)** 60 62.

Lithuania defeated Iceland 3-0:
Gvidas Sabeckis **(LTU)** d. Andri Jonsson **(ISL)** 62 62; Alvaras Balzekas **(LTU)** d. Arnar Sigursson **(ISL)** 61 36 63; Rolandas Murashka/Gvidas Sabeckis **(LTU)** d. David Halldorsson/Andri Jonsson **(ISL)** 62 61.

Final Positions: 1. Monaco, 2. Andorra, 3. Turkey, 4. Bosnia & Herzegovina, 5. Lithuania, 6. Namibia, 7. Iceland, 8. Botswana.

Monaco and Andorra promoted to Euro/African Zone Group II in 2003. Iceland and Botswana relegated to Euro/African Zone Group IV in 2003.

Euro/African Zone – Venue II

Date: 8-12 May Venue: Gdynia, Poland Surface: Clay (O)
Group A: Estonia, Mauritius, Madagascar
Group B: Cyprus, FYR Macedonia, Poland, Cyprus

Group A

8 May Madagascar defeated Mauritius 3-0:
Donne-Dubert Radison (MAD) d. Ananda Sawmynaden (MRI) 60 61; Alexis Rafidison (MAD) d. Jean-Marcel Bourgault du Coudray (MRI) 63 76(1); Dubert Rafidison/Jean-Marc Randriamanalina (MAD) d. Jean-Marcel Bourgault du Coudray/Ananda Sawmynaden (MAD) 67(6) 62 61;

9 May Estonia defeated Mauritius 3-0:
Andrei Luzgin (EST) d. Ananda Sawmynaden (MRI) 63 61; Rene Busch (EST) d. Jean-Marcel Bourgault du Coudray (MRI) 62 62; Andres Angejarv/Ivar Troost (EST) d. Jean-Marcel Bourgault/Ananda Sawmynaden (MRI) 61 64.

10 May Estonia defeated Madagascar 2-1:
Andrei Luzgin (EST) d. Donne-Dubert Radison (MAD) 64 64; Alexis Rafidison (MAD) d. Rene Busch (EST) 60 62; Andrei Luzgin/Ivar Troost (EST) d. Alexis Rafidison/Jean-Marc Randriamanalina (MAD) 16 62 75.

Group B

8 May Poland defeated Cyprus 3-0:
Bartlomiej Dabrowski (POL) d Dinos Pavlou (CYP) 60 60; Mariusz Fyrstenberg (POL) d. Marcos Baghdatis (CYP) 46 63 62; Bartlomiej Dabrowski/Lukasz Kubot (POL) d. Marcos Baghdatis/Petros Baghdatis (CYP) 64 76(3).

FYR Macedonia defeated Tunisia 2-1:
Zoran Sevcenko (MKD) d. Heithen Abid (TUN) 63 62; Oualid Jallali (TUN) d. Predrag Rusevski (MKD) 61 60; Predrag Rusevski/Zoran Sevcenko (MKD) d. Issam Jallali/Oualid Jallali (TUN) 63 63.

9 May Poland defeated FYR Macedonia 3-0:
Bartlomiej Dabrowski (POL) d. Kristijan Mitrovski (MKD) 61 60; Mariusz Fyrstenberg (POL) d. Predrag Rusevski (MKD) 64 62; Lukasz Kubot/Filip Urban (POL) d. Dimitar Grabulovski/Predrag Rusevski (MKD) 62 63.

Tunisia defeated Cyprus 2-1:
Heithem Abid (TUN) d. Dinos Pavlou (CYP) 62 62; Oualid Jallali (TUN) d. Marcos Baghdatis (CYP) 75 62; Marcos Baghdatis/Petros Baghdatis (CYP) d. Heithem Abid/Oualid Jallali (TUN) 64 26 62.

10 May Poland defeated Tunisia 2-1:
Bartlomiej Dabrowski (POL) d. Heithem Abid (TUN) 62 61; Oualid Jallali (TUN) d. Mariusz Fyrstenberg (POL) 75 64; Bartlomiej Dabrowski/Lukasz Kubot (POL) d. Heithem Abid/Malek Jaziri (TUN) 63 64.

Cyprus defeated FYR Macedonia 2-1:
Dinos Pavlou (CYP) d. Zoran Sevcenko (MKD) 64 63; Marcos Baghdatis (CYP) d. Predrag Rusevski (MKD) 75 61; Predrag Rusevski/Zoran Sevcenko (MKD) d. Marcos Baghdatis/Petros Baghdatis (CYP) 57 63 75.

Playoff for 1st-4th Positions:
Results carried forward:
Poland defeated Tunisia 2-1;
Estonia defeated Madagascar 2-1.

11 May Poland defeated Madagascar 3-0:
Bartlomiej Dabrowski (POL) d. Donne-Dubert Radison (MAD) 60 60; Lukasz Kubot (POL) d. Alexis Rafidison (MAD) 62 60; Mariusz Fyrstenberg/Filip Urban (POL) d. Donne-Dubert Radison/Jean-Marc Randriamanalina (MAD) 75 62.

Tunisia defeated Estonia 2-1:
Andrei Luzgin (EST) d. Heithem Abid (TUN) 63 36 64; Oualid Jallali (TUN) d. Rene Busch (EST) 63 61; Issam Jallali/Oualid Jallali (TUN) d. Andrei Luzgin/Ivar Troost (EST) 46 63 1816.

12 May Poland defeated Estonia 3-0:
Bartlomiej Dabrowski (POL) d. Andres Angerjarv (EST) 60 60; Lukasz Kubot (POL) d. Ivar Troost (EST) 63 62; Mariusz Fyrstenberg/Filip Urban (POL) d. Andres Angerjarv/Andrei Luzgin (EST) 64 60.

Tunisia defeated Madagascar 3-0:
Heithem Abid (TUN) d. Jean-Marc Randriamanalina (MAD) 64 76(5); Oualid Jallali (TUN) d. Donne-Dubert Radison (MAD) 60 61; Issam Jallali/Malek Jaziri (TUN) d. Donne-Dubert Radison/Jean-Marc Randriamanalina (MAD) 61 62.

Playoff for 5th-7th Positions:
Result carried forward:
Cyprus defeated FYR Macedonia 2-1.

11 May FYR Macedonia defeated Mauritius 3-0:
Zoran Sevcenko (MKD) d. Ananda Sawmynaden (MRI) 61 61; Predrag Rusevski (MKD) d. Jean-Marcel Bourgault du Coudray (MRI) 64 76(4); Dimitar Grabulovski//Kristijan Mitrovski (MKD) defeated Jean-Marcel Bourgault du Coudray/Ananda Sawmynaden (MRI) 64 60.

12 May Cyprus defeated Mauritius 3-0:
Dinos Pavlou (CYP) d. Ananda Sawmynaden (MRI) 62 63; Marcos Baghdatis (CYP) d. Jean-Marcel Bourgault du Coudray (MRI) 64 61; Petros Baghdatis/ Eleftherios Christou (CYP) d. Ananda Sawmynaden/Arnaud Serret (MRI) 61 61.

Final Positions: 1. Poland, 2. Tunisia, 3. Estonia, 4. Madagascar, 5. Cyprus, 6. FYR Macedonia, 7. Mauritius.

Poland and Tunisia promoted to Euro/African Zone Group II in 2003. Mauritius relegated to Euro/African Zone Group IV in 2003.

American Zone

Date: 1-7 April Venue: San Salvador, El Salvador Surface: Clay (O)
Group A: Dominican Republic, El Salvador, Panama, Puerto Rico
Group B: Costa Rica, Haiti, Honduras, Jamaica

Group A

3 April El Salvador defeated Puerto Rico 2-1:
Jose Baires (ESA) d. Luis Haddock (PUR) 62 63; Gabriel Montilla (PUR) d. Manuel Tejada (ESA) 76(2) 64; Jose Baires/Augusto Sanabria (ESA) d. Ricardo Jordan/Gabriel Montilla (PUR) 63 46 75.

Dominican Republic defeated Panama 3-0:
Juan Berrido (DOM) d. Arnulfo Courtney (PAN) 63 61; Victor Estrella (DOM) d. Chad Valdez (PAN) 62 63; Jose Bernal/Victor Estrella (DOM) d. Braen Aneiros/John Silva (PAN) 63 62.

4 April Dominican Republic defeated El Salvador 2-1:
Jose Baires (ESA) d. Juan Berrido (DOM) 62 16 63; Victor Estrella (DOM) d. Manuel Tejada (ESA) 64 61; Jose Bernal/Victor Estrella (DOM) d. Jose Baires/Augusto Sanabria (ESA) 76(5) 64.

Puerto Rico defeated Panama 2-1:
Arnulfo Courtney (PAN) d. Nicolas Lopez (PUR) 62 64; Gabriel Montilla (PUR) d. Chad Valdez (PAN) 75 62; Ricardo Jordan/ Gabriel Montilla (PUR) d. Braen Aneiros/Chad Valdez (PAN) 63 64.

5 April El Salvador defeated Panama 3-0:
Jose Baires (ESA) d. Braen Aneiros (PAN) 62 61; Manuel Tejada (ESA) d. Chad Valdez (PAN) 62 10 ret; Augusto Sanabria/Manuel Tejada (ESA) d. Braen Aneiros/John Silva (PAN) 64 64.

Puerto Rico defeated Dominican Republic 2-1:
Juan Berrido (DOM) d. Luis Haddock (PUR) 64 62; Gabriel Montilla (PUR) d. Victor Estrella (DOM) 62 61; Ricardo Jordan/ Gabriel Montilla (PUR) d. Jose Bernal/Victor Estrella (DOM) 64 76(1).

Group B

3 April Jamaica defeated Costa Rica 3-0:
Ryan Russell (JAM) d. Juan Carlos Gonzalez (CRC) 63 60; Scott Willinsky (JAM) d. Federico Camacho (CRC) 64 62; Jermaine Smith/ Damar Johnson (JAM) d. David Alvarado/Diego Alvarado (CRC) 76(4) 62.

Haiti defeated Honduras 2-1:
Bertrand Madsen (HAI) d. Calton Alvarez (HON) 61 63; Carlos Caceres (HON) d. Iphton Louis (HAI) 62 75; Bertrand Madsen/ Iphton Louis (HAI) d. Carlos Caceres/Pablo Hernandez (HON) 76(6) 61.

4 April Jamaica defeated Honduras 3-0:
Ryan Russell (JAM) d. Calton Alvarez (HON) 61 60; Scott Willinsky (JAM) d. Carlos Caceres (HON) 64 64; Damar Johnson/Jermaine Smith (JAM) d. Franklin Garcia/Pablo Hernandez (HON) 63 76(7).

Haiti defeated Costa Rica 3-0:
Bertrand Madsen (HAI) d. David Alvarado (CRC) 61 62; Iphton Louis (HAI) d. Federico Camacho (CRC) 61 76(5); Joel Allen/Carl-Henry Barthold (HAI) d. Diego Alvarado/Federico Camacho (CRC) 63 26 63.

5 April Haiti defeated Jamaica 2-1:
Bertrand Madsen (HAI) d. Ryan Russell (JAM) 62 75; Iphton Louis (HAI) d. Scott Willinsky (JAM) 64 76(4); Damar Johnson/Jermaine Smith (JAM) d. Joel Allen/Carl-Henry Barthold (HAI) 63 75.

Honduras defeated Costa Rica 3-0:
Calton Alvarez (HON) d. Juan Carlos Gonzalez (CRC) 62 63; Carlos Caceres (HON) d. Federico Camacho (CRC) 63 64; Franklin Garcia/Pablo Hernandez (HON) d. Diego Alvarado/Federico Camacho (CRC) 64 57 63.

Playoff for 1st-4th Positions:
Results carried forward:
Dominican Republic defeated El Salvador 2-1;
Haiti defeated Jamaica 2-1.

6 April Dominican Republic defeated Jamaica 2-1:
Ryan Russell (JAM) d. Juan Berrido (DOM) 64 63; Victor Estrella (DOM) d. Scott Willinsky (JAM) 76(3) 61; Jose Bernal/Victor Estrella (DOM) d. Damar Johnson/Jermaine Smith (JAM) 75(5) 64.

Haiti defeated El Salvador 2-1:
Bertrand Madsen (HAI) d. Jose Baires (ESA) 62 63; Manuel Tejada (ESA) d. Iphton Louis (HAI) 57 62 61; Joel Allen/Bertrand Madsen (HAI) d. Jose Baires/Augusto Sanabria (ESA) 63 36 1412.

7 April Dominican Republic defeated Haiti 3-0:
Jose Bernal (DOM) d. Carl-Henry Barthold (HAI) 63 64; Victor Estrella (DOM) d. Ipthon Louis (HAI) 62 76(1); Jose Bernal/Jose Antonio Velazquez (DOM) d. Joel Allen/Carl Henry Barthold (HAI) 67(6) 64.

Jamaica defeated El Salvador 2-1:
Augusto Sanabria (ESA) d. Damar Johnson (JAM) 36 63 64; Scott Willinsky (JAM) d. Manuel Tejada (ESA) 76(4) 64; Damar Johnson/Scott Willinskiy (JAM) d. Jaime Cuellar/Augusto Sanabria (ESA) 62 64.

Playoff for 5th-8th Positions:
Results carried forward:
Puerto Rico defeated Panama 2-1;
Honduras defeated Costa Rica 3-0.

6 April Honduras defeated Panama 3-0:
Calton Alvarez (HON) d. Arnulfo Courtney (PAN) 76(1) 64; Carlos Caceres (HON) d. Chad Valdez (PAN) 63 75; Franklin Garcia/Pablo Hernandez (HON) d. Braen Aneiros/Chad Valdez (PAN) 63 63.

Puerto Rico defeated Costa Rica 3-0:
Luis Haddock (PUR) d. David Alvarado (CRC) 76(2) 63; Gabriel Montilla (PUR) d. Federico Camacho (CRC) 60 76(7); Ricardo Jordan/Gabriel Montilla (PUR) d. David Alvarado/Diego Alvarado (CRC) 63 62.

7 April Costa Rica defeated Panama 2-1:
David Alvarado (CRC) d. John Silva (PAN) 75 26 64; Juan Carlos Gonzalez (CRC) d. Braen Aneiros (PAN) 57 61 86; Braen Aneiros/John Silva (PAN) d. Diego Alvarado/Juan Carlos Gonzalez (CRC) w/o.

Honduras defeated Puerto Rico 3-0:
Calton Alvarez (HON) d. Ricardo Jordan (PUR) 63 67(3) 60; Carlos Caceres (HON) d. Nicolas Lopez (PUR) 62 61; Franklin Garcia/Pablo Hernandez (HON) d. Ricardo Jordan/Nicolas Lopez (PUR) 64 75.

Final Positions: 1. Dominican Republic, 2. Haiti, 3. Jamaica, 4. El Salvador, 5. Honduras, 6. Puerto Rico, 7. Costa Rica, 8. Panama.

Dominican Republic and Haiti promoted to American Zone Group II in 2003.
Costa Rica and Panama relegated to American Zone Group IV in 2003.

Asia/Oceania Zone
Date: 10-14 April Venue: Tehran, Iran Surface: Clay (O)
Group A: Iran, Qatar, Singapore, United Arab Emirates
Group B: Syria, Saudi Arabia, Pacific Oceania, Tajikistan

Group A
10 April Iran defeated Qatar 3-0:
Anoosha Shahgholi (IRI) d. Sultan-Khalfan Al Alawi (QAT) 62 75; Akbar Taheri (IRI) d. Nasser-Ghanim Al Khulaifi (QAT) 62 61; Ashkan Shokoofi/Akbar Taheri (IRI) d. Mohammed Al Kuwari/Mohammed-Ali Al Saoud (QAT) 62 62.

United Arab Emirates defeated Singapore 3-0:
Mahmoud Nader (UAE) d. Yuan-Xiong Hiu (SIN) 76(3) 57 86; Omar Bahrouzyan (UAE) d. Jonathan Kam (SIN) 75 62; Omar Bahrouzyan/ Mahmoud Nader (UAE) d. Andrew Kam/Jonathan Kam (SIN) 75 57 62.

11 April Iran defeated United Arab Emirates 3-0:
Shahab Hassani-Nafez (IRI) d. Mahmoud Nader (UAE) 63 62; Anoosha Shahgholi (IRI) d. Omar Bahrouzyan (UAE) 67(5) 62 60; Ashkan Shokoofi/Akbar Taheri (IRI) d. Omar Bahrouzyan/ Mahmoud Nader (UAE) 61 62.

Qatar defeated Singapore 3-0:
Sultan-Khalfan Al Alawi (QAT) d. Yuan-Xiong Hiu (SIN) 60 61; Nasser-Ghanim Al Khulaifi (QAT) d. Andrew Kam (SIN) 63 62; Mohammed Al Kuwari/Mohammed-Ali Al Saoud (QAT) d. Yuan-Xiong Hiu/Andrew Kam (SIN) 67(2) 75 97.

12 April Iran defeated Singapore 3-0:
Shahab Hassani-Nafez (IRI) d. Andrew Kam (SIN) 64 61; Akbar Taheri (IRI) d. Jonathan Kam (SIN) 60 60; Anoosha Shahgholi/Ashkan Shokoofi (IRI) d. Andrew Kam/Jonathan Kam (SIN) 62 61.

United Arab Emirates d. Qatar 2-1:
Sultan-Khalfan Al Alawi (QAT) d. Mahmoud Nader (UAE) 62 60; Omar Bahrouzyan (UAE) d. Nasser-Ghanim Al Khulaifi (QAT) 46 64 62; Omar Bahrouzyan/Mahmoud Nader (UAE) d. Sultan-Khalfan Al Alawi/Nasser-Ghanim Al Khulaifi (QAT) 63 63.

Group B
10 April Tajikistan defeated Syria 2-1:
Mansour Yakhyaev (TJK) d. Laith Salim (SYR) 63 62; Rabi Bou-Hassoum (SYR) d. Sergei Makashin (TJK) 63 63; Sergei Makashin/ Mansour Yakhyaev (TJK) d. Rabi Bou-Hassoum/Laith Salim (SYR) 64 75.

Pacific Oceania defeated Saudi Arabia 2-1:
Leon So'onalole (POC) d. Bader Al-Megayel (KSA) 46 75 108; Omar Al-Mogayel (KSA) d. Brett Baudinet (POC) 67(6) 64 75; Brett Baudinet/Juan Sebastien Langton (POC) d. Bader Al Megayel/Baqer Abu Khulaif (KSA) 26 63 1412.

11 April Syria defeated Saudi Arabia 2-1:
Bader Al Megayel (KSA) d. Laith Salim (SYR) 36 63 119; Rabi Bou-Hassoum (SYR) d. Omar Al Thagib (KSA) 63 61; Rabi Bou-Hassoum/Laith Salim (SYR) d. Bader Al Megayel/Baqer Abu Khulaif (KSA) 64 64.

Tajikistan defeated Pacific Oceania 2-1:
Mansour Yakhyaev (TJK) d. Leon So'onalole (POC) 36 62 75; Sergei Makashin (TJK) d. Brett Baudinet (POC) 61 62; Brett Baudinet/Juan Sebastien Langton (POC) d. Sergei Makashin/Mansour Yakhyaev (TJK) 57 63 86.

12 April Pacific Oceania defeated Syria 2-1:
Juan Sebastien Langton (POC) d. Laith Salim (SYR) 06 61 1412; Rabi Bou-Hassoum (SYR) d. Leon So'onalole (POC) 76(5) 62; Rabi Bou-Hassoum/Raher Maghzoumeh (SYR) d. Brett Baudinet/Juan Sebastien Langton (POC) 63 61.

Tajikistan defeated Saudi Arabia 2-1:
Mansour Yakhyaev (TJK) d. Baqer Abu Khulaif (KSA) 67(9) 62 60; Sergei Makashin (TJK) d. Bader Al Megayel (KSA) 64 76(1); Omar Al Thagib/Baqer Abu Khulaif (KSA) d. Sergei Makashin/Mansour Yakhyaev (TJK) 21 ret.

Playoff for 1st-4th Positions:
Results carried forward:
Iran defeated United Arab Emirates 3-0;
Tajikistan defeated Pacific Oceania 2-1.

13 April Iran defeated Pacific Oceania 2-1:
Anoosha Shahgholi (IRI) d. Leon So'onalole (POC) 64 63; Akbar Taheri (IRI) d. Brett Baudinet (POC) 60 75; Brett Baudinet/Juan Sebastien Langton (POC) d. Ashkan Shokoofi/Akbar Taheri (IRI) 76(8) 36 63.

Tajikistan defeated United Arab Emirates 3-0:
Mansour Yakhyaev (TJK) d. Mahmoud Nader (UAE) 64 63; Sergei Makashin (TJK) d. Omar Bahrouzyan (UAE) 75 26 63; Sergei Makashin/Mansour Yakhyaev (TJK) d. Mahmoud Nader/Ali Sherif (UAE) 62 60.

14 April United Arab Emirates defeated Pacific Oceania 2-1:
Leon So'onalole (POC) d. Mahmoud Nader (UAE) 63 62; Omar Bahrouzyan (UAE) d. Brett Baudinet (POC) 16 63 63; Mahmoud Nader/Omar Bahrouzyan (UAE) d. Juan Sebastien Langton/Leon So'onalole (POC) 63 64.

Iran defeated Tajikistan 3-0:
Anoosha Shahgholi (IRI) d. Mansour Yakhyaev (TJK) 62 64; Akbar Taheri (IRI) d. Sergei Makashin (TJK) 64 63; Anoosha Shahgholi/Shahab Hassani-Nafez (IRI) d. Sergei Makashin/Mansour Yakhyaev (TJK) 75 63.

Playoff for 5th-8th Positions:
Results carried forward:
Qatar defeated Singapore 3-0;
Syria defeated Saudi Arabia 2-1.

13 April Qatar defeated Saudi Arabia 2-1:
Sultan-Khalfan Al Alawi (QAT) d. Baqer Abu Khulaif (KSA) 60 63; Bader Al Megayel (KSA) d. Nasser-Ghanim Al Khulaif (QAT) 76(2) 46 75; Sultan-Khalfan Al Alawi/Mohammed-Ali Al Saoud (QAT) d. Bader Al Megayel/Omar Al Thagib (KSA) 64 61.

Syria defeated Singapore 2-1:
Laith Salim (SYR) d. Yuan-Xiong Hiu (SIN) 46 64 64; Rabi Bou-Hassoum (SYR) d. Andrew Kam (SIN) 64 63; Yuan-Xiong Hiu/Andrew Kam (SIN) d. Rabi Bou-Hassoum/Raher Maghzoumeh (SYR) 65 ret.

14 April Qatar defeated Syria 2-1:
Sultan-Khalfan Al Alawi (QAT) d. Abraham Ibrahim (SYR) 64 61; Rabi Bou-Hassoum (SYR) d. Mohammed-Ali Al Saoud (QAT) 61 62; Sultan-Khalfan Al Alawi/Mohammed Al Kuwari (QAT) 46 61 63.

Singapore defeated Saudi Arabia 2-1:
Yuan-Xiong Hiu (SIN) d. Bader Al Megayel (KSA) 75 62; Omar Al Thagib (KSA) d. Andrew Kam (SIN) 26 75 62; Yuan-Xiong Hiu/Andrew Kam (SIN) d. Baqer Abu Khulaif/Omar Al Thagib (KSA) 64 67(5) 61.

Final Positions: 1. Iran, 2. Tajikistan, 3. United Arab Emirates, 4. Pacific Oceania, 5. Qatar, 6. Syria, 7. Singapore, 8. Saudi Arabia.

Iran and Tajikistan promoted to Asia/Oceania Zone Group II in 2003.
Singapore and Saudi Arabia relegated to Asia/Oceania Zone Group IV in 2003.

GROUP IV

Euro/African Zone – Venue 1

Date: 6-10 February Venue: Mombasa, Kenya Surface: Hard (O)
Group A: Djibouti, Kenya, Rwanda
Group B: Algeria, Angola, Ethiopia, Malta

Group A
6 February Kenya defeated Rwanda 3-0:
Norbert Oduor (KEN) d. Eric Hagenimana (RWA) 61 62; Trevor Kiruki (KEN) d. Sylvain Rutikanga (RWA) 62 64; Trevor Kiruki/Francis-Mwangi Rogoi (KEN) d. Eric Hagenimana/Alain Hakizimana (RWA) 64 63.

7 February Rwanda defeated Djibouti 3-0:
Jean-Claude Gasigwa (RWA) d. Abdourahman-Omar Aden (DJI) 61 61; Eric Hagenimana (RWA) defeated Hamdi-Aden Moussa (DJI) 61 61; Jean-Claude Gasigwa/Alain Hakizimana (RWA) d. Abdourahman-Omar Aden/Mahfoud Mouktar (DJI) 63 60.

8 February Kenya defeated Djibouti 3-0:
Francis-Mwangi Rogoi (KEN) d. Mounawar-Bourhan Ali (DJI) 60 61; Norbert Oduor (KEN) d. Hamdi-Aden Moussa (DJI) 60 60; Trevor Kiruki/Francis-Mwangi Rogoi (KEN) d. Mounawar-Bourhan Ali/Hamdi-Aden Moussa (DJI) 60 60.

Group B
6 February Algeria defeated Ethiopia 3-0:
Lamine Ouahab (ALG) d. Elias Mukember (ETH) 61 60; Abdelhak Hameurlaine (ALG) d. Yohannes Setegnwandimu (ETH) 62 60; Sofiane Dob/Noureddine Mahmoudi (ALG) d. Mikaile Asfaw/Yohannes Setegnwandimu (ETH) 57 75 62.

Angola defeated Malta 3-0:
Jose Nenganga (ANG) d. Mark Schembri (MLT) 46 63 86; Nelson De Almeida (ANG) d. Maurizio Cappello (MLT) 64 62; Joao-Sebastiao Miguel/Jose Nenganga (ANG) d. Maurizio Cappello/Marcus Delicata (MLT) 64 76(3).

7 February Algeria defeated Malta 3-0:
Lamine Ouahab (ALG) d. Mark Schembri (MLT) 62 60; Noureddine Mahmoudi (ALG) d. Marcus Delicata (MLT) 62 60; Sofiane Dob/Abdelhak Hameurlaine (ALG) d. Maurizio Cappello/Mark Schembri (MLT) 62 61.

Angola defeated Ethiopia 3-0:
Jose Nenganga (ANG) d. Mikaile Asfaw (ETH) 64 75; Nelson De Almeida (ANG) d. Yohannes Setegnwandimu (ETH) 64 61; Joao-Sebastiao Miguel/Jose Nenganga (ANG) d. Habtamu Gebrekidan/Elias Mukember (ETH) 64 61.

8 February Algeria defeated Angola 2-1:
Lamine Ouahab (ALG) d. Jose Nenganga (ANG) 60 63; Nelson De Almeida (ANG) d. Abdelhak Hameurlaine (ALG) 64 16 62; Noureddine Mahmoudi/Lamine Ouahab (ALG) d. Nelson De Almeida/Joao-Sebastiao Miguel (ANG) 60 62.

Malta defeated Ethiopia 3-0:
Mark Schembri (MLT) d. Mikaile Asfaw (ETH) 64 63; Marcus Delicata (MLT) d. Yohannes Setegnwandimu (ETH) 46 63 86; Marcus Delicata /Mark Schembri (MLT) d. Asfaw/Elias Mukember (ETH) 63 57 62.

Playoff for 1st-4th Positions:
Results carried forward:
Kenya defeated Rwanda 3-0;
Algeria defeated Angola 2-1.

9 February Algeria defeated Rwanda 3-0:
Lamine Ouahab (ALG) d. Eric Hagenimana (RWA) 62 62; Noureddine Mahmoudi (ALG) d. Sylvain Rutikanga (RWA) 61 62; Sofiane Dob/Noureddine Mahmoudi (ALG) d. Jean-Claude Gasigwa/Alain Hakizimana (RWA) 62 46 64.

Angola defeated Kenya 2-1:
Jose Nenganga (ANG) d. Trevor Kiruki 61 64; Nelson De Almeida (ANG) d. Allan Cooper 36 63 86; Trevor Kiruki/Norbert Oduor (KEN) d. Joao-Sebastiao Miguel/Jose Nenganga (ANG) 36 63 64.

10 February Algeria defeated Kenya 3-0:
Lamine Ouahab (ALG) d. Trevor Kiruki (KEN) 64 64; Abdelhak Hameurlaine (ALG) d. Allan Cooper (KEN) 46 76(5) 60; Abdelhak Hameurlaine/Lamine Ouahab (ALG) d. Trevor Kiruki/ Francis-Mwangi Rogoi (KEN) 63 62.

Angola defeated Rwanda 3-0:
Jose Nenganga (ANG) d. Jean-Claude Gasigwa (RWA) 57 60 61; Nelson De Almeida (ANG) d. Eric Hagenimana (RWA) 64 75; Nelson De Almeida/Joao-Sebastiao Miguel d. Alain Hakizimana/Sylvain Rutikanga (RWA) 64 61.

Playoff for 5th-7th Positions:
Result carried forward:
Malta defeated Ethiopia 3-0.

9 February Malta defeated Djibouti 3-0:
Mark Schembri (MLT) d. Mounawar-Bourhan Ali (DJI) 60 60; Marcus Delicata (MLT) d. Mahfoud Mouktar (DJI) 61 60; Marcus Delicata/Mark Schembri (MLT) d. Abdourahman-Omar Aden/Mahfoud Mouktar (DJI) 60 60.

10 February Ethiopia defeated Djibouti 3-0:
Habtamu Gebrekidan (ETH) d. Mahfoud Mouktar (DJI) 60 62; Elias Mukember (ETH) d. E.Mukember d. Hamdi-Aden Moussa 60 61; Mikaile Asfaw/Yohannes Setegnwandimu d. Abdourahman-Omar Aden/Mahfoud Mouktar (DJI) 61 60.

Final Positions: 1. Algeria, 2. Angola, 3. Kenya, 4. Rwanda, 5. Malta, 6. Ethiopia, 7. Djibouti.

Algeria and Angola promoted to Euro/Africa Zone Group III in 2003.

Euro/African Zone – Venue 2

Date: 12-16 June Venue: San Marino Surface: Clay (O)
Nations: Azerbaijan, Georgia, Liechtenstein, Nigeria, San Marino, Uganda

12 June San Marino defeated Nigeria 2-1:
Massimiliano Rosti (SMR) d. Abdul-Mumin Babalolo (NGR) 63 63; Domenico Vicini (SMR) d. Rotimi Jegede (NGR) 61 36 61; Toyin Dairo/Sunday Maku (NGR) d. Christian Rosti/Domenico Vicini (SMR) 46 76(4) 65.

Azerbaijan defeated Liechtenstein 2-1:
Stephan Ritter (LIE) d. Farid Shirinov (AZE) 62 61; Emin Aghayev (AZE) d. Jurgen Tomordy (LIE) 61 62; Emin Aghayev/Farid Shirinov (AZE) d. Stephan Ritter/Herbert Weirather (LIE) 63 46 64.

Georgia defeated Uganda 3-0:
Vladimir Kakulia (GEO) d. Godfrey Uzunga (UGA) 62 63; Irakli Ushangishvili (GEO) d. Charles Yokwe (UGA) 61 60; Vladimir Gabrichidze/Irakli Ushangishvili (GEO) d. Godfrey Uzunga/Charles Yokwe (UGA) 62 63.

13 June San Marino defeated Uganda 3-0:
Massimiliano Rosti (SMR) d. Christopher Baagala (UGA) 61 61;
Domenico Vicini (SMR) d. Godfrey Uzunga (UGA) 62 63; William
Forcellini/Christian Rosti (SMR) d. Christopher Baagala/Godfrey
Uzunga (UGA) 62 36 62.

Georgia defeated Liechtenstein 2-1:
Herbert Weirather (LIE) d. Vladimir Kakulia (GEO) 63 57 64;
Irakli Ushangishvili (GEO) d. Jurgen Tomordy (LIE) 62 64; Vladimir
Gabrichidze/Irakli Ushangishvili (GEO) d. Kenny Banzer/Stephan
Ritter (LIE) 60 60.

Azerbaijan defeated Nigeria 2-1:
Rotimi Jegede (NGR) d. Farid Shirinov (AZE) 75 63; Emin Aghayev
(AZE) d. Sunday Maku (NGR) 62 61; Emin Aghayev/Farid Shirinov
(AZE) d. Abdul-Mumin Babalola/Toyin Dairo (NGR) 63 64.

14 June Azerbaijan defeated San Marino 2-1:
Massimiliano Rosti (SMR) d. Farid Shirinov (AZE) 60 60; Emin
Aghayev (AZE) d. Domenico Vicini (SMR) 60 61; Emin Aghayev/
Farid Shirinov (AZE) d. Christian Rosti/Domenico Vicini (SMR)
63 60.

Nigeria defeated Georgia 2-1:
Rotimi Jegede (NGR) d. Vladimir Gabrichidze (GEO) 75 31 Ret;
Irakli Ushangishvili (GEO) d. Sunday Maku (NGR) 62 61; Abdul-
Mumin Babalola/Sunday Maku (NGR) d. Vladimir Gabrichidze/
Irakli Ushangishvili (GEO) 64 46 75.

Liechtenstein defeated Uganda 3-0:
Stephan Ritter (LIE) d. Patrick Olobo (UGA) 62 62; Herbert
Weirather (LIE) d. Christopher Baagala (UGA); Kenny Banzer/Jurgen
Tomordy (LIE) d. Christopher Baagala/Patrick Olobo (UGA) 60 62.

15 June Georgia defeated San Marino 3-0:
Vladimir Kakulia (GEO) d. Massimiliano Rosti (SMR) 57 64 62;
Irakli Ushangishvili (GEO) d. Domenico Vicini (SMR) 36 63 64;
Vladimir Gabrichidze/Vladimir Kakulia (GEO) d. William Forcellini/
Christian Rosti (SMR) 62 64.

Nigeria d. Liechtenstein 2-1:
Stephan Ritter (LIE) d. Abdul-Mumin Babalola (NGR) 64 67(6) 64;
Rotimi Jegede (NGR) d. Herbert Weirather (LIE) 63 64; Abdul-
Mumin Babalola/ Sunday Maku (NGR) d. Stephan Ritter/Jurgen
Tomordy (LIE) 64 61.

Azerbaijan defeated Uganda 2-1:
Farid Shirinov (AZE) d. Godfrey Uzunga (UGA) 76(4) 63; Emin
Aghayev (AZE) d. Charles Yokwe (UGA) 60 62; Godfrey Uzunga/
Charles Yokwe (UGA) d. Talat Rahimov/Farid Shirinov (AZE)
36 76(4) 75.

16 June San Marino defeated Liechtenstein 2-0:
Massimiliano Rosti (SMR) d. Stephan Ritter (LIE) 76(6) 76(1);
Domenico Vicini (SMR) d. Jurgen Tomordy (LIE) 46 76(3) 63;
William Forcellini/ Christian Rosti (SMR) vs Kenny Banzer/Jurgen
Tomordy (LIE) – not played.

Nigeria defeated Uganda 3-0:
Rotimi Jegede (NGR) d. Godfrey Uzunga (UGA) 75 61; Sunday
Maku (NGR) d. Charles Yokwe (UGA) 62 64; Rotimi Jegede/Sunday
Maku (NGR) d. Christopher Baagala/Patrick Olobo (UGA) 61 61.

Georgia defeated Azerbaijan 2-1:
Vladimir Kakulia (GEO) d. Talat Rahimov (AZE) 64 62; Irakli
Ushangishvili (GEO) d. Farid Shirinov (AZE) 63 75; Talat
Rahimov/Farid Shirinov (AZE) d. Vladimir Kakulia/Irakli
Ushangishvili (GEO) 61 63.

Final Positions: 1. Georgia, 2. Azerbaijan, 3. San Marino,
4. Nigeria, 5. Liechtenstein, 6. Uganda.

*Georgia and Azerbaijan promoted to Euro/African Zone Group III
in 2003.*

American Zone

**Date: 1-6 April Venue: Kingstown, St. Vincent & Grenadines Surface:
Hard (O)**
Nations: Barbados, Bermuda, Bolivia, Eastern Caribbean States,
St. Lucia, US Virgin Islands

1 April Bolivia defeated Eastern Caribbean States 3-0:
Alberto Sottocorno (BOL) d. Dexter Christian (ECA) 63 63; Javier
Taborga (BOL) d. Glynn James (ECA) 61 75; Alberto Sottocorno/
Gonzalo Ulloa (BOL) d. Hayden Ashton/Glynn James (ECA)
36 75 86.

Bermuda defeated US Virgin Islands 2-1:
Janson Bascome (BER) d. John Richards (ISV) 64 62;
Eugene Highfield (ISV) d. James Collieson (BER) 62 61;
Janson Bascome/James Collieson (BER) d. Eugene Highfield/
John Richards (ISV) 64 36 63.

St. Lucia defeated Barbados 3-0:
Vernon Lewis (LCA) d. Jonathan Lewis (BAR) 61 62; Kane Easter
(LCA) d. James Betts (BAR) 60 61; Sirsean Arlain/Yves Sinson (LCA)
d. Damien Applewhaite/Haydn Lewis (BAR) 75 76(2).

2 April Bermuda defeated Eastern Caribbean States 2-1:
Janson Bascome (BER) d. Christian Dexter (ECA) 26 63 63; Glynn
James (ECA) d. James Collieson (BER) 36 60 61; Janson
Bascome/James Collieson (BER) d. Hayden Ashton/Glynn James
(ECA) 76(4) 61.

Bolivia defeated St. Lucia 2-1:
Vernon Lewis (LCA) d. Alberto Sottocorno (BOL) 75 63; Javier
Taborga (BOL) d. Kane Easter (LCA) 63 64; Alberto Sottocorno/
Javier Taborga (BOL) d. Kane Easter/Yves Sinson (LCA)
64 76(4).

Barbados defeated US Virgin Islands 3-0:
Jonathan Lewis (BAR) d. John Richards (ISV) 60 60; James Betts
(BAR) d. Eugene Highfield (ISV) 63 64; Damien Applewhaite/Haydn
Lewis (BAR) d. John Richards/Bruce Wray (ISV) 75 62.

**3 April Eastern Caribbean States defeated US Virgin Islands
3-0:**
Dexter Christian (ECA) d. John Richards (ISV) 62 63; Glynn James
(ECA) d. Eugene Highfield (ISV) 34 ret.; Hayden Ashton/Deron
Grant (ECA) d. John Richards/Bruce Wray (ISV) 62 63.

Bolivia defeated Barbados 3-0:
Alberto Sottocorno (BOL) d. Jonathan Lewis (BAR) 76(6) 63; Javier
Taborga (BOL) d. James Betts (BAR) 62 62; Alberto Sottocorno/ Javier
Taborga (BOL) d. Damien Applewhaite/Haydn Lewis (BAR) 63 60.

St. Lucia defeated Bermuda 2-1:
Vernon Lewis (LCA) d. Janson Bascome (BER) 64 62; James
Collieson (BER) d. Kane Easter (LCA) 64 36 62; Vernon Lewis/Yves
Sinson (LCA) d. Janson Bascome/James Collieson (BER) 75 63.

5 April St. Lucia defeated Eastern Caribbean States 3-0:
Sirsean Arlain (LCA) d. Deron Grant 46 75 75 (ECA); Vernon Lewis
(LCA) d. Glynn James (ECA) 62 60; Sirsean Arlain/Yves Sinson (LCA)
d. Hayden Ashton/Glynn James 36 63 62.

Bermuda defeated Barbados 2-1:
Janson Bascome (BER) d. Jonathan Lewis (BAR) 76(7) 57 62;
James Collieson (BER) d. Damien Applewhaite (BAR) 63 62;
Damien Applewhaite/ Haydn Lewis (BAR) d. Janson Bascome/
James Collieson (BER) 57 76(6) 64.

Bolivia defeated US Virgin Islands 3-0:
Gonzalo Ulloa (BOL) d. John Richards (ISV) 61 61; Javier Taborga
(BOL) d. Eugene Highfield (ISV) 57 61 61; Alberto Sottocorno/
Javier Taborga (BOL) d. John Richards/Bruce Wray (ISV) 62 60.

6 April Barbados defeated Eastern Caribbean States 3-0:
Haydn Lewis (BAR) d. Dexter Christian (ECA) 61 63; Damien
Applewhaite (BAR) d. Glynn James (ECA) 62 46 86; James Betts/
Jonathan Lewis (BAR) d. Hayden Ashton/Deron Grant 61 57 61.

St. Lucia defeated US Virgin Islands 3-0:
Yves Sinson (LCA) d. John Richards (ISV) 62 46 62; Vernon Lewis
(LCA) d. Eugene Highfield (ISV) 62 61; Vernon Lewis/Yves Sinson
(LCA) d. Eugene Highfield/John Richards (ISV) 64 61.

Bolivia defeated Bermuda 2-1:
Janson Bascome (BER) d. Gonzalo Ulloa (BOL) 57 61 61; Alberto
Sottocorno (BOL) d. James Collieson (BER) 64 46 60; Alberto
Sottocorno/Gonzalo Ulloa (BOL) d. Ryan Swan/Jovan Whitter (BER)
63 63.

Final Positions: 1. Bolivia, 2. St. Lucia, 3. Bermuda,
4. Barbados, 5. Eastern Caribbean States, 6. US Virgin Islands

*Bolivia and St Lucia promoted to American Zone Group III in
2003.*

Asia/Oceania Zone

Date: 20-24 March Venue: Dhaka, Bangladesh Surface: Hard (O)
Group A: Bahrain, Brunei, Iraq, Kyrgyzstan
Group B: Bangladesh, Jordan, Oman, Sri Lanka

Group A

20 March Kyrgyzstan defeated Iraq 2-1:
Sadam-Hussain Kadhim **(IRQ)** d. Ruslan Eshmuhamedov **(KGZ)** 75 63; Eduard Koifman **(KGZ)** d. Kadhim-Hussain Kadhim **(IRQ)** 64 57 61; Ruslan Eshmuhamedov/Eduard Koifman **(KGZ)** d. Haider-Hussain Kadhim/Husain-Ahmed Rashid **(IRQ)** 46 61 75.

Bahrain defeated Brunei 2-1:
Abdul Rahman Shehab **(BRN)** d. Tan Chok **(BRU)** 63 61; Esam Abdulaal **(BRN)** d. Billy Wong **(BRU)** 60 61; Tan Chok/Billy Wong **(BRU)** d. Omar-Mohamed Ahmed/Al-Sayed Ismaeel **(BRN)** 36 64 61.

21 March Kyrgyzstan defeated Bahrain 2-1:
Ruslan Eshmudamedov **(KGZ)** d. Abdul Rahman Shehab **(BRN)** 63 76(7); Eduard Koifman **(KGZ)** d. Esam Abdulaal **(BRN)** 60 64; Al-Sayed Ismaeel/ Abdul Rahman Shehab **(BRN)** d. Ernest Batyrbekov/Ilia Sazonov **(KGZ)** 60 61.

Iraq defeated Brunei 3-0:
Haider-Hussain Kadhim **(IRQ)** d. Ian Chok **(BRU)** 62 62; Sadam-Hussain Kadhim **(IRQ)** d. Billy Wong **(BRU)** 46 62 61; Husain-Ahmed Rashid/Sadam-Hussain Kadhim **(IRQ)** d. Ian Chok/Billy Wong **(BRU)** 62 60.

22 March Bahrain defeated Iraq 2-1:
Abdul Rahman Shehab **(BRN)** d. Haider-Hussain Kadhim **(IRQ)** 76(2) 46 64; Esam Abdulaal **(BRN)** d. Sadam-Hussain Kadhim **(IRQ)** 36 62 64; Kadhim-Hussain Kadhim/Husain-Ahmed Rashid **(IRQ)** d. Al-Sayed Ismaeel/Abdul Rahman Shehab **(BRN)** 76(6) 63.

Kyrgyzstan defeated Brunei 3-0:
Ruslan Eshmuhamedov **(KGZ)** d. Izannie Abu-Bakar **(BRU)** 60 60; Eduard Koifman **(KGZ)** d. Ian Chok **(BRU)** 60 62; Ernest Batyrbekov/Ilia Sazonov **(KGZ)** d. Izannie Abu-Bakar/Pg Hj Mohamed Ridzuan **(BRU)** 60 60.

Group B

20 March Bangladesh defeated Oman 3-0:
Shibu Lal **(BAN)** d. Khalid Al-Nabhani **(OMA)** 63 64; Hira Lal **(BAN)** d. Mohammed Al-Nabhani **(OMA)** 67(7) 62 60; Shibu Lal/Dilip Passia **(BAN)** d. Khalid Al-Nabhani/Mohammed Al-Nabhani **(OMA)** 64 46 75.

Sri Lanka defeated Jordan 2-1:
Fabio Badra **(JOR)** d. Franklyn Emmanuel **(SRI)** 63 75; Rajeev Rajapakse **(SRI)** d. Ahmad Al Hadid **(JOR)** 46 62 30 ret.; Franklyn Emmanuel/Rajeev Rajapakse **(SRI)** d. Ahmad Al Hadid/Fabio Badra **(JOR)** 62 64.

21 March Bangladesh defeated Jordan 3-0:
Shibu Lal **(BAN)** d. Fabio Badra **(JOR)** 64 61; Hira Lal **(BAN)** d. Ahmad Al Hadid **(JOR)** 62 10 ret.; Shibu Lal/Dilip Passia **(BAN)** d. Fabio Badra/Tareq Shkakwa **(JOR)** 63 61.

Oman defeated Sri Lanka 2-1:
Mudrik Al-Rawahi **(OMA)** d. Franklyn Emmanuel **(SRI)** 67(5) 62 64; Rajeev Rajapkse **(SRI)** d. Khalid Al-Nabhani **(OMA)** 76(4) 62; Khalid Al-Nabhani/Mohammed Al-Nabhani **(OMA)** d. Franklyn Emmanuel/Rajeev Rajapakse **(SRI)** 61 75.

22 March Sri Lanka defeated Bangladesh 2-1:
Shibu Lal **(BAN)** d. Harshana Godamanna **(SRI)** 62 61; Rajeev Rajapakse **(SRI)** d. Dilip Passia **(BAN)** 67(5) 62 61; Franklyn Emmanuel/Rajeev Rajapakse **(SRI)** d. Shibu Lal/Dilip Passia **(BAN)** 76(6) 64.

Oman defeated Jordan 3-0:
Mudrik Al-Rawahi **(OMA)** d. Tareq Shkakwa **(JOR)** 61 63; Khalid Al-Nabhani **(OMA)** d. Fabio Badra **(JOR)** 76(1) 75; Khalid Al-Nabhani/Mohammed Al-Nabhani **(OMA)** d. Fabio Badra/Tareq Shkakwa **(JOR)** 61 62.

Playoff for 1st-4th Positions:
Results carried forward:
Kyrgyzstan defeated Bahrain 2-1;
Bangladesh defeated Oman 3-0.

23 March Bahrain defeated Bangladesh 2-1:
Shibu Lal **(BAN)** d. Abdul Rahman Shehab **(BRN)** 63 62; Esam Abdulaal **(BRN)** d. Hira Lal **(BAN)** 64 62; Esam Abdulaal/Abdul Rahman Shehab **(BRN)** d. Shibu Lal/Hira Lal **(BAN)** 62 63.

Oman defeated Kyrgyzstan 2-1:
Ruslan Eshmuhamedov **(KGZ)** d. Khalid Al-Nabhani **(OMA)** 62 63; Mohammed Al-Nabhani **(OMA)** d. Eduard Koifman **(KGZ)** 62 46 64; Khalid Al-Nabhani/Mohammed Al-Nabhani **(OMA)** d. Ruslan Eshmuhamedov/ Eduard Koifman **(KGZ)** 60 76(7).

24 March Kyrgyzstan defeated Bangladesh 3-0:
Ruslan Shmoukhamedov **(KGZ)** d. Shibu Lal **(BAN)** 62 64; Eduard Koifman **(KGZ)** d. Dilip Passia **(BAN)** 61 62; Ruslan Shmoukhamedov/Eduard Koifman **(KGZ)** d. Amol Roy/Shibu Lal **(BAN)** 64 16 61.

Bahrain defeated Oman 3-0:
Abdul-Rayman Shehab **(BRN)** d. Khalid Al-Nabhani **(OMA)** 62 61; Essam Abdul-Aal **(BRN)** d. Mohammed Al-Nabhani **(OMA)** 64 64; Omar-Mohammed Ahmed/Al-Sayad Ismael **(BRN)** d. Mudrik Al-Rawahi/Saleh Al-Zadjali **(OMA)** 60 62.

Playoff for 5th-8th Positions:
Results carried forward:
Iraq defeated Brunei 3-0;
Sri Lanka defeated Jordan 2-1.

23 March Iraq defeated Jordan 2-1:
Husain-Ahmed Rashid **(IRQ)** d. Tareq Shkakwa **(JOR)** 61 61; Fabio Badra **(JOR)** d. Haider-Hussain Kadhim **(IRQ)** 64 63; Haider-Hussain Kadhim/ Husain-Ahmed Rashid **(IRQ)** d. Fabio Badra/Tareq Shkakwa **(JOR)** 62 63.

Sri Lanka defeated Brunei 3-0:
Franklyn Emmanuel **(SRI)** d. Ian Chok **(BRU)** 62 63; Rajeev Rajapakse **(SRI)** d. Billy Wong **(BRU)** 61 62; Harshana Godamanna/Oshada Wijemanne **(SRI)** d. Ian Chok/Billy Wong **(BRU)** 63 60.

24 March Sri Lanka defeated Iraq 2-1:
Husain-Ahmed Rashid **(IRQ)** d. Franklyn Emmanuel **(SRI)** 76(4) 62; Rajeev Rajapakse **(SRI)** d. Haider-Hussain Kadhim **(IRQ)** 63 60; Franklyn Emmanuel/Rajeev Rajapakse **(SRI)** d. Haider-Hussain Kadhim/Husain-Ahmed Rashid **(IRQ)** 60 61.

Jordan defeated Brunei 3-0:
Tareq Shkakwa **(JOR)** d. Ian Chok **(BRU)** 75 64; Fabio Badra **(JOR)** d. Billy Wong Loong **(BRU)** 62 64; Fabio Badra/Tareq Shkakwa **(JOR)** d. Ian Chok/Billy Wong Loong **(BRU)** 76(8) 64.

Final Positions: 1. Kyrgyzstan, 2. Bahrain, 3. Bangladesh, 4. Oman, 5. Sri Lanka, 6. Iraq, 7. Jordan, 8. Brunei

Kyrgyzstan and Bahrain promoted to Asia/Oceania Zone Group III in 2003.

Writing a book like this would not be possible without the able assistance of so many friends and colleagues in the fascinating global tennis world. First, and foremost, thanks to the International Tennis Federation and their Head of Communications, Barbara Travers for their continued trust and support with this project.

The participants have delivered rich and fulsome colour to my year and I'd like to express special gratitude to those who have given of their time, be they players or captains, in alphabetical order: Jonas Bjorkman, James Blake, Guillermo Canas, Arnaud Clement, Alex Corretja, Thomas Enqvist, Roger Federer, John Fitzgerald, Guy Forget, Sebastien Grosjean, Gaston Gaudio, Carl-Axel Hageskog, Tim Henman, Goran Ivanisevic, Thomas Johansson, Yevgeny Kafelnikov, Ivan Ljubicic, Xavier Malisse, Patrick McEnroe, Jiri Novak, Andrei Pavel, Andy Roddick, Greg Rusedski, Pete Sampras, Fabrice Santoro and Roger Taylor.

Many thanks, of course, to The Times' Head of Sport Keith Blackmore and Sports Editor, David Chappell for embracing this project and lending their whole-hearted support; to my fellow tennis-writing itinerants, especially the enduringly excellent Philippe Bouin of L'Equipe, Alfredo Bernardi of La Nacion in Argentina, and Neven Bertecevic from Croatia. Best wishes, of course, to all my colleagues from Britain.

I must apologize again to those great people from ATP Communications, who put up with me saying 'Davis Cup interview please' every hour of the day and night. To Nicola Arzani, Benito Perez-Barbadillo, J.J. Carter, Martin Dagahs, David Massey, and the indefatigable Greg Sharko, much gratitude. Thanks, too, to Jon Friend of TPL.

Untold thanks to Barbara and her team at the ITF, especially Nick Imison for keeping me on my toes and editing with such wisdom and enthusiasm. To Randy Walker at the USTA, Heidi Cohu at the British LTA and Stephan Brun of the FFT and their staff, special felicitations.

To Maureen, Elizabeth and Kathleen, much love and many kisses.

Neil Harman, December 3, 2002.

Ron Angle:
11, 12/13, 25, 26, 27, 51, 52, 53, 54, 55

Dmitri Astakhov:
35, 36, 37

Dusan Barbus:
84, 85

Sergio Carmona:
19, 20, 21

Giannia Ciaccia:
23 (bottom right)

Arne Forsell/Bildbyran:
14, 16, 17, 18, 56, 58, 59,

Andrei Golovanov:
42/43

Andrei Golovanov and Sergei Kivrin:
10, 70, 72, 73, 74, 75, 76

Tommy Hindley/Professional Sport:
80, 81, 96

Vincent Kalut/Photo News:
86, 87

Henk Koster:
90, 91

Daniel Maurer:
32, 34, 40/41

Fred and Susan Mullane:
62/63, 64, 66, 67, 68, 69

Susan Mullane:
28, 29, 30, 31, 44, 45, 46, 47, 60

Andy Muller:
88, 89

Serge Philippot:
23 (left/top right), 24, 48, 49, 50

Marcelo Ruschel:
38, 39, 78/79, 94, 95

Paul Zimmer:
4, 6, 8, 9, 82, 83, 98/99, 100, 101, 102, 103, 104, 105, 106, 107, 108, 109, 110, 111, 112, 113, 114, 115, 116